The Australian Women's Weekly cookbooks

There's no reason why any of us shouldn't indulge in a spot of wicked eating from time to time... and what better way to go than with chocolate, cream and a hundred other sweet treats. These days, we're so besieged with low-fat, no-fat, lite and fat-free foods that a little dining decadence is good for the soul... and, in moderation, not really too bad for the body either. So, relax, live a little and immerse yourself in these amazingly delicious Wicked Sweet Indulgences!

Pamela Clark

Food Director

contents

get wicked

One of the best things about these wicked indulgences (besides being both wicked and indulgent) is that they're not difficult to make. With a little background to start you on the right track and some helpful tips to keep you on the road to success, the trip to presenting an impressive looking and delicious tasting cake, biscuit or dessert to an appreciative audience can be an enjoyable, and easy, journey.

After you select the recipe you want to make from this book, it's important you read the recipe right to the end, so that you're not surprised by calls for a 3-hour refrigeration time or one really important ingredient which sadly isn't residing in your pantry or refrigerator. Make certain you've left yourself time to make the recipe without having to hurry; mistakes happen when you cook under pressure.

Twist paper into a cone shape

BAKING

1 Oven types and rack positions

There are many types of ovens and energy sources so it is important that you "get to know your oven", particularly when it comes to baking. The recipes in this book requiring baking were tested in domestic-sized electric ovens; none were cooked in a microwave or microwave/convection oven as baking times and results would be different from conventionally baked items.

If using a fan-forced oven, check the operating instructions for best results. As a rule, reduce the temperature by 10°C to 20°C when using the fan during baking, and be aware that baking times might be slightly less than specified. Some ovens give better results if the fan is introduced about halfway through the baking time.

Position the oven racks and cake pan(s) so that the top of the baked item is roughly in the centre of the oven. Several items can be baked at the same time, either on the same or different racks, providing the pans do not touch each other, or the oven wall or door, to allow for even circulation of heat. To ensure even browning, cake pans on different racks should exchange positions about halfway through baking time; move the lower items to the top rack, and vice versa. This will not affect the baked item if you do it gently and quickly.

Best results are obtained by baking in an oven preheated to the desired temperature; this usually takes about 10 minutes. This rule is particularly important for items that bake in less than 30 minutes.

In most cases we used aluminium cake pans because they give the best results for baking. Cake pans made from materials having various coatings, such as non-stick, work well providing the surface is unscratched. Pans made from tin and stainless steel do not conduct heat as evenly as aluminium; lower your oven temperature slightly (about 10°C) when using cake pans other than aluminium.

oven temperatures

These oven temperatures are only a guide. Always check the manufacturer's manual.

	°C (Celsius)	°F (Fahrenheit)	Gas Mark
Very slow	120	250	1
Slow	150	300	2
Moderately slow	160	325	3
Moderate	180 - 190	350 - 375	4
Moderately hot	200 - 210	400 - 425	5
Hot	220 - 230	450 - 475	6
Very hot	240 - 250	500 - 525	7

Staple the cone to hold its shape

Plastic bags are particularly useful for piping chocolate

2 How to prepare cake pans

To grease a cake pan or tin, use either a light, even coating of a cooking-oil spray, or a pastry brush to brush melted butter or margarine evenly over the base and side(s). Sometimes recipes call for a greased and floured cake pan. Simply grease the pan evenly (melted butter is best in this case) and allow it to "set" a minute or two before sprinkling a little flour evenly over the greased area. Tap the pan several times on your bench then tip out the excess flour.

Cakes that are high in sugar, or that contain golden syrup, treacle or honey, have a tendency to stick so we recommend lining the base and/or side(s) of their pans. Trace around the base of the pan with a pencil onto greaseproof or baking paper; cut out the shape, slightly inside the pencil mark, so the paper fits snugly over the base of the greased pan. It is not necessary to grease the baking paper once it is in position.

3 To test if a cake is cooked

All cake-baking times are approximate. Check your cake at the suggested cooking time; it should be browned and starting to shrink from the side(s) of the pan. Feel the top with your fingertips – it should feel firm.

In all cakes except a sponge, you can try inserting a thin skewer (we prefer to use a metal skewer rather than a wooden one because any mixture that adheres to it is easier to see) into the deepest part of the cake from top to base. Gently remove the skewer: it shouldn't have any uncooked mixture clinging to it. Do not confuse cake mixture with stickiness from fruit.

4 Cooling cakes

We have suggested standing cakes for various times before turning onto wire racks to cool further. The best way to do this, after standing time has elapsed, is to hold the cake pan firmly and shake it gently, thus loosening the cake. Turn the cake, upside down, onto a wire rack, then turn the cake top-side up immediately using a second rack (unless directed otherwise).

We have indicated when it is best to cool cakes in the pans in which they were baked; generally, fruit cakes are the type cooled in this way, and these should always be covered with foil before cooling.

5 Making piping bags

You can make your own piping bag from greaseproof or baking paper, or a small plastic bag. To make a paper piping bag, cut a 30cm square of the paper in half diagonally, twist into a cone shape. Staple or fold the cone to hold its shape. Half-fill the cone with frosting, cream or cooled melted chocolate, etc., then fold the top edges of the cone over themselves to keep the contents contained. Snip a tiny bit from the tip of the cone, and pipe by holding the bag firmly, and applying even pressure.

Stir melting chocolate gently between bursts of microwave power

Grate chocolate on a hand grater

Plastic bags are particularly useful for piping chocolate. Place chocolate, before melting, in the same small microwave-safe plastic bag you plan on using as a piping bag. Tuck open end of bag under, place in microwave oven; heat on MEDIUM power (55%), for 15- to 20-second intervals until chocolate is melted. Carefully remove from microwave oven; cool slightly. Ease chocolate down into one bottom corner of the bag; twist top of bag to hold chocolate securely. Snip a tiny bit off the corner of the bag to pipe chocolate.

6 Tips and tricks

• We do not advise mixing cakes in blenders or processors unless specified in individual recipes. Use an electric beater to mix cakes and slices, and always have the ingredients at room temperature, particularly the butter. Melted or extremely soft butter will alter the texture of the baked item.
• Start mixing ingredients on a low speed; once combined, increase the speed to about medium and beat for the required time. Creamed mixtures for cakes can be mixed with a wooden spoon, but it takes a lot longer.
• When measuring liquids, always stand the marked measuring jug on a flat surface and check at eye level for accuracy.
• Spoon and cup measurements should be levelled off with a knife or spatula. Be careful when measuring ingredients such as honey or treacle.

7 How to keep cakes, biscuits, etc.

Most cakes, biscuits and slices keep well for two or three days, depending on the ambient climate and type of sweet but, as a rule, remember that the higher the fat content, the longer your wicked indulgence will keep. Make sure cakes and biscuits are at room temperature before storing in an airtight container as close in size to the item as possible; this minimises the amount of air around the item.

CHOCOLATE TECHNIQUES
How to melt chocolate

Please note that melting and tempering chocolate is not the same thing. Tempering chocolate subjects it to specific temperatures and techniques which result in the particular texture and sheen seen in fine chocolate sweets and pâtisserie.

Melting chocolate is not difficult if you follow a few rules. Everything you use when melting chocolate, from the pan to the stirring spoon to your hands, must be absolutely dry: the slightest amount of water in the chocolate will cause it to seize, that is, clump and turn an unappealing grey colour. Even an extremely humid day can affect the results. The second problem in melting chocolate is excessive or direct heat.

No matter what method you choose to melt chocolate, patience and following directions are the two most important guidelines. Don't cut corners to save time.

Use a vegetable peeler to make small chocolate curls

Scrape a flat knife across chocolate to make large curls

Microwave-oven method
Place coarsely chopped chocolate in a small microwave-safe bowl; heat on MEDIUM power (55%), for 15- to 20-second intervals, pausing to stir gently between times. The chocolate will hold its shape even after it's melted, so the stirring is important. When the chocolate is almost melted, remove from the microwave oven and allow it to sit a minute or two to complete the melting process.

Cooktop method
This method takes more time but there is less to do than if using the microwave-oven method. Place a little water in a small saucepan – make sure the water won't touch the bottom of your choice of small heatproof bowl (a glass or china bowl is best) when it is fitted inside the pan. Cover pan and bring the water to a boil. Remove lid from pan; sit bowl, uncovered, over the simmering water until chocolate is melted, stirring from time to time.

After chocolate has melted, carefully remove the bowl of chocolate and wipe underside of the container with a dry tea-towel.

How to grate chocolate
Be sure that the piece of chocolate you intend to grate is cool and firm. Grate on hand grater, cleaning the grater often so that the chocolate doesn't clog the surface of the blade. You can also "grate" chocolate in a blender – this is especially good if you're grating a lot of chocolate – but be sure to chop the chocolate coarsely first.

How to store chocolate
Chocolate should be stored in cool, dry conditions; if it becomes too warm, the cocoa butter rises to the surface and forms a slightly grey film known as "bloom". This is not harmful and, once the chocolate is melted, it will usually return to its natural deep-brown colour. If chocolate is refrigerated

or frozen, bring it to room temperature before using. You will soon discover that chocolate is very sensitive to temperature change and you have to always keep the weather, room temperature, the heat from your hands, etc., in mind when dealing with chocolate.

Making chocolate curls
Using a sharp vegetable peeler, scrape along the side of a long piece of room-temperature eating-quality chocolate.

For larger curls, spread melted chocolate evenly and thinly onto clean flat oven tray, cutting board or, ideally, a piece of marble; stand until just set but not hard. Scrape a flat knife across chocolate, pulling curls off with every movement. If the curls start to resemble shavings, the chocolate is too cold. Curls can be stored in an airtight container at room temperature until required (if the weather is hot, keep them in the refrigerator).

Brush any sugar grains from the side of the saucepan   *Use a candy thermometer for accurate results*

SUGAR-SYRUP BASICS

Making your own toffee, nougat and fudge is both fun and satisfying – you'll find yours are much more delicious than store-bought! And it doesn't have to be difficult if you...

• Always use the recommended size saucepan – a larger or smaller pan will affect both quality and cooking time.

• Don't try to halve or double the recipe – decreasing or increasing the quantities of ingredients will affect the cooking time and most likely cause the recipe to fail.

• Make the sugar-syrup on a cool, dry day if possible because excessive heat or humidity can have an effect on the outcome. On a really humid day, cook sugar syrup to a temperature a degree or two higher than the recipe indicates.

• To prevent crystallisation or graininess, the sugar must be dissolved completely; brush down any grains that cling to the side of the saucepan. After sugar syrup has come to a boil, do not stir it, and do not scrape the pan or stir during cooling.

• A candy thermometer is a necessity if you intend to frequently make sweets such as nougat and fudge. Most thermometers can reach temperatures between 30°C (60°F) and 200°C (400°F) and are a cheap yet crucial tool when making anything that requires a specific degree of heat.

• Choose a thermometer that is easy to handle when dealing with hot mixtures. A good thermometer should have a stainless steel body, and an adjustable clip or hook enabling it to be attached to your pan. The most accurate thermometers are the ones that hold the bulb securely up and away from the pan's base.

• Before you begin to make your recipe, test your thermometer by placing it in a small saucepan of cold water; bring the water to a boil. An accurate thermometer will display 100°C (212°F). If the reading is higher or lower, take this difference into account when testing the temperature of whatever you're cooking; for example, if your thermometer reads 98°C (208°F) when the water boils, then you'll have to adjust your mixture's reading by 2°C (4°F).

• When reading the temperature on your thermometer, your eyes should be at the same height as the mercury level. Looking at the thermometer from a different angle can result in an incorrect reading. Watch the temperature closely once it reaches 90°C because it can escalate quite rapidly. For an accurate reading, the candy thermometer should stand upright in the substance, not touching the base of the pan.

Pour toffee onto an oven tray to make toffee shards

Use a zester to remove rind when making crystallised rind

• Do not allow the candy
thermometer to sit in the
mixture after it has reached
the desired temperature
(unless the recipe states
otherwise). After you have
finished using it, place the
thermometer back in a saucepan
of boiling water, remove the pan
from the heat and allow the water
to cool with the thermometer
in it, thus decreasing the
temperature gradually.
• Wash and dry the cold
thermometer carefully, wrap
in a cloth, and keep in a
safe place where it won't be
bumped or broken.
• After you have made
your toffee, the best way to
clean the pan is to fill it
with enough water to cover
any remaining toffee then
simmer, covered, over medium
heat, until all the toffee
has melted from the pan's
base and side. Wash and dry
the pan in the normal way.

To make toffee shards
After toffee has reached the
correct temperature or is the
colour required, remove the pan
from the heat, allow the bubbles
to subside then pour the hot
toffee onto a lightly oiled
oven tray; do not scrape the
toffee from the pan, or it might
crystallise. Allow toffee to set
at room temperature; break into
shards with hands.

To spin toffee
Lightly grease two oven trays;
after your toffee has reached
the correct temperature or is
the desired colour, remove the
pan from the heat. Allow all of
the bubbles to subside from the
toffee before using it. Dip two
clean forks into the toffee and,
working quickly, pull and spin
the toffee backwards and forwards
between the forks, over the
trays. It is best to use the
spun toffee within 1 hour
for decorating.

To make crystallised rind
Using the citrus fruit of your
choice, you can make crystallised
rind several hours before required
if you keep it, covered, at
room temperature.
    Using a vegetable peeler,
remove the rind from fruit; peel
rind as thinly as possible to avoid
taking any of the bitter white
pith. Reserve the fruit for another
use; citrus fruit will keep up to
a week in the refrigerator after
having been peeled.
    Using a sharp vegetable knife,
cut the rind into thin strips. Place
½ cup (110g) caster sugar in small
saucepan; add ¼ cup (60ml) water,
stir over heat, without boiling, until
sugar dissolves. Add the rind; simmer,
without stirring, for 5 minutes.
    Remove rind from syrup with
metal tongs, spread onto a wire
rack to cool before using.
    Alternatively, use a zester to
thinly peel the rind from the fruit,
then proceed making the sugar
syrup as above.

desserts

white-choc panna cotta with passionfruit sauce

PREPARATION TIME 20 MINUTES (plus refrigeration time) • COOKING TIME 10 MINUTES

Panna cotta translates from the Italian as "cooked cream", but this dessert is far more delectable than these simple words. Sauternes is a dessert wine from the region of the same name in western France. You will need approximately six passionfruit for this recipe.

300ml thickened cream

³/₄ cup (180ml) milk

150g white chocolate, chopped coarsely

¹/₃ cup (75g) caster sugar

2 teaspoons gelatine

1 tablespoon water

¹/₂ cup (125ml) passionfruit pulp

1 cup (250ml) Sauternes-style dessert wine

1 Grease six ¹/₂-cup (125ml) non-metallic moulds.

2 Combine cream, milk, chocolate and 2 tablespoons of the sugar in small saucepan; stir over heat, without boiling, until smooth.

3 Sprinkle gelatine over the water in small heatproof jug. Stand jug in small saucepan of simmering water; stir until gelatine dissolves. Stir into cream mixture.

4 Divide mixture among prepared moulds; refrigerate, covered, about 3 hours or until set.

5 Meanwhile, combine passionfruit, wine and remaining sugar in small saucepan. Bring to a boil; reduce heat. Simmer, uncovered, without stirring, about 10 minutes or until passionfruit syrup reduces by a third; cool.

6 Turn panna cotta onto serving plates; drizzle with passionfruit syrup.

SERVES 6

tips Panna cotta can be made a day ahead and refrigerated, covered. Serve the remaining dessert wine with the panna cotta.

passionfruit, also known as granadilla, adds a refreshing taste to desserts with its tropical, tangy flavour

mini apple charlottes with caramel sauce

PREPARATION TIME 25 MINUTES • COOKING TIME 30 MINUTES

*We used Granny Smith apples here, but another variety, such as
Golden Delicious, is an acceptable substitute.*

1 Grease four 1-cup (250ml) metal moulds.

2 Peel and core apples; cut into thin wedges. Cook apple with
sugar and juice in large frying pan, stirring until apple browns
and mixture bubbles and thickens.

3 Preheat oven to hot. Remove crusts from bread slices. Cut one
5.5cm round from each of four bread slices; cut remaining bread
slices into three strips each. Brush one side of each round and strip
with butter. Place one round, buttered-side down, in each mould;
line side of each mould with bread strips, buttered-side against side
of mould, slightly overlapping edges. Firmly pack warm apple mixture
into moulds. Fold end of each bread strip down into centre of charlotte
to enclose filling; press firmly to seal.

4 Place moulds on oven tray; bake, uncovered, in hot oven about
15 minutes or until charlottes are golden brown. Turn, top-side up,
onto serving plates; drizzle with caramel sauce.

caramel sauce Melt butter in small frying pan. Add sugar; stir until
dissolved. Add juice; cook, stirring, until sauce thickens slightly.

SERVES 4

tips It's best if you use sliced raisin bread that's a few days old.
You can also use plain white bread instead of the raisin bread.

4 large apples (800g)
**1/4 cup (50g) firmly packed
 brown sugar**
1/4 cup (60ml) orange juice
1 loaf sliced raisin bread (560g)
80g butter, melted

CARAMEL SAUCE

50g butter
**1/2 cup (100g) firmly packed
 brown sugar**
1/3 cup (80ml) orange juice

Stir apples until mixture thickens

Line side of mould with bread slices

Fold bread to enclose filling

chocolate hazelnut self-saucing puddings

PREPARATION TIME 15 MINUTES • COOKING TIME 25 MINUTES

Nutella is a commercial spread made of milk chocolate and hazelnuts; it can be used in cooking, as here, or spread on your breakfast toast.

1/2 cup (125ml) milk

40g dark chocolate, chopped coarsely

50g butter

1/3 cup (35g) cocoa powder

1/2 cup (75g) self-raising flour

1/4 cup (25g) hazelnut meal

1/3 cup (75g) caster sugar

2/3 cup (150g) firmly packed brown sugar

1 egg, beaten lightly

3/4 cup (180ml) water

40g butter, chopped, extra

200g vanilla ice-cream

CHOCOLATE HAZELNUT SAUCE

1/2 cup (125ml) cream

2 tablespoons brown sugar

50g dark chocolate, chopped finely

1/3 cup (110g) Nutella

1 tablespoon Frangelico

1 Preheat oven to moderate. Grease four 1-cup (250ml) ovenproof dishes.

2 Stir milk, chocolate, butter and half of the cocoa in small saucepan over low heat until smooth.

3 Combine flour, hazelnut meal, caster sugar and half of the brown sugar in medium bowl. Add chocolate mixture and egg; stir until combined. Divide mixture among prepared dishes.

4 Stir the water, extra butter, remaining brown sugar and remaining cocoa in small saucepan over low heat until smooth. Pour hot mixture gently and evenly over puddings; bake puddings, uncovered, in moderate oven about 25 minutes. Stand 5 minutes; top with ice-cream then chocolate hazelnut sauce.

chocolate hazelnut sauce Combine cream and sugar in small saucepan. Bring to a boil; remove from heat. Add chocolate; stir until smooth. Add Nutella and liqueur; stir until smooth.

SERVES 4

tip This dessert is best served hot because the sauce is quickly absorbed by the puddings.

the hazelnut-flavoured liqueur, Frangelico, can also be served along with cups of espresso next to these puddings

mini pecan, macadamia and walnut pies

PREPARATION TIME 20 MINUTES (plus refrigeration time)
COOKING TIME 25 MINUTES

1 Grease four 10cm-round loose-based flan tins.

2 Blend or process flour, sugar and almond meal with butter until combined. Add egg yolk; process until ingredients just come together. Knead pastry on floured surface until smooth. Cover with plastic wrap; refrigerate 30 minutes.

3 Divide pastry into quarters. Roll each piece, between sheets of baking paper, into rounds large enough to line prepared tins; lift pastry into each tin. Press into sides; trim edges. Cover; refrigerate 1 hour.

4 Preheat oven to moderately hot. Place tins on oven tray; line each tin with baking paper then fill with uncooked rice or dried beans. Bake, uncovered, in moderately hot oven 10 minutes; remove paper and rice. Bake further 7 minutes or until pastry cases are browned lightly; cool.

5 Reduce oven temperature to moderate. Divide filling among cases. Bake in moderate oven about 25 minutes or until set; cool.

filling Combine ingredients in medium bowl; mix well.

SERVES 4

tips Uncooked rice or dried beans used to weigh down the pastry during blind-baking are not suitable for eating. You can use them every time you bake-blind; after cooling, keep them in an airtight jar.
Do not use maple-flavoured syrups as a substitute for the "real thing" in the nut filling.

1¹/₄ cups (185g) plain flour
¹/₃ cup (55g) icing sugar mixture
¹/₄ cup (30g) almond meal
125g cold butter, chopped
1 egg yolk

FILLING
¹/₃ cup (50g) macadamias, toasted
¹/₃ cup (35g) pecans, toasted
¹/₃ cup (35g) walnuts, toasted
2 tablespoons brown sugar
1 tablespoon plain flour
40g butter, melted
2 eggs, beaten lightly
³/₄ cup (180ml) maple syrup

Press pastry around each tin's side

Fill lined pastry with uncooked rice

Divide filling equally among cases

passionfruit and coconut crème brûlée

PREPARATION TIME 15 MINUTES (plus refrigeration time) • COOKING TIME 40 MINUTES

The English, Spanish and French all stake a claim in the origin of crème brûlée; wherever it came from, the fact remains that it is a universal favourite. You will need approximately six passionfruit for this recipe.

2 eggs
4 egg yolks
1/4 cup (55g) caster sugar
1/2 cup (125ml) passionfruit pulp
12/3 cups (400ml) coconut cream
300ml thickened cream
2 tablespoons brown sugar

1 Preheat oven to moderate.

2 Combine eggs, egg yolks, caster sugar and passionfruit in medium heatproof bowl.

3 Combine coconut cream and cream in small saucepan; bring to a boil. Gradually whisk hot cream mixture into egg mixture. Place bowl over medium saucepan of simmering water; stir over heat about 10 minutes or until custard mixture thickens slightly and coats the back of a spoon.

4 Divide custard among eight 1/2-cup (125ml) heatproof dishes or cups. Place dishes in large baking dish. Pour enough boiling water into baking dish to come halfway up sides of dishes; bake in moderate oven about 20 minutes or until custards just set. Remove custards from water; cool to room temperature. Cover; refrigerate 3 hours or overnight.

5 Place custards in shallow flameproof dish filled with ice cubes; sprinkle each with 1 teaspoon brown sugar. Using finger, distribute sugar over surface of each custard, pressing in gently; place under preheated hot grill until tops of crème brûlées are caramelised.

SERVES 8

tip Preheat grill on highest setting for about 5 minutes. It's important the sugar on the custards browns as quickly as possible (the ice in the baking dish helps keep the custards cold while the sugar is caramelising).

Whisk hot cream mixture into egg mixture

Drag a finger across spoon to test custard has thickened

Press sugar gently into surface of brûlées

ripe cherry cheesecake

PREPARATION TIME 30 MINUTES (plus refrigeration time)
COOKING TIME 50 MINUTES

Originally called a Black Forest Cherry Torte because it contained whole cherries and cherry brandy (kirsch), our version of this German extravaganza uses a well-known chocolate sweet instead – but remains just as delightfully wicked!

1 Grease 24cm springform tin.

2 Blend or process biscuits until mixture resembles fine breadcrumbs. Add butter; process until just combined. Using one hand, press biscuit mixture evenly over base of prepared tin. Cover; refrigerate about 30 minutes or until firm.

3 Preheat oven to moderate.

4 Meanwhile, beat cheese and sugar in medium bowl with electric mixer until smooth; add eggs, one at a time, beating well between additions. Gradually beat in chocolate; fold Cherry Ripe and cherries into cheesecake mixture.

5 Place tin on oven tray. Spread cheesecake mixture into tin; bake in moderate oven about 50 minutes or until set. Remove from oven; cool to room temperature. Cover; refrigerate 3 hours or overnight.

6 Serve cheesecake decorated with chocolate roses, if desired.

SERVES 10

tips Use absorbent paper to soak up liquid from the cherries. Chocolate should be cool, but not set, before it is added to the cheesecake mixture.

To make chocolate roses, melt your choice of chocolate then spread evenly over marble or a foil covered surface. When chocolate is almost set, drag ice-cream scoop over surface of chocolate to make roses.

125g plain chocolate biscuits
75g butter, melted
2 x 250g packets cream
    cheese, softened
1/3 cup (75g) caster sugar
2 eggs
200g dark chocolate, melted
2 x 85g Cherry Ripe bars,
    chopped coarsely
425g can seeded black cherries in
    syrup, drained

Dry the drained cherries well

Press biscuit mixture into base of pan

Drag scoop over chocolate to make roses

lemon curd crepe cake

PREPARATION TIME 30 MINUTES (plus refrigeration time) • COOKING TIME 40 MINUTES

This cake is best assembled a day before serving. You need approximately three large lemons for this recipe.

3/4 cup (110g) plain flour
3 eggs
1 tablespoon vegetable oil
1¹/₃ cups (330ml) milk
2 teaspoons finely grated
   lemon rind
3/4 cup (180ml) lemon juice
1¹/₂ cups (330g) caster sugar
6 eggs, beaten lightly, extra
125g butter, chopped
2 teaspoons gelatine
2 tablespoons water

1 Line base and side of deep 20cm-round cake pan with plastic wrap.

2 Place flour in medium bowl; make well in centre. Gradually whisk in combined eggs, oil and milk; strain batter into large jug. Cover; stand crepe batter 30 minutes.

3 Heat greased crepe pan or small heavy-based non-stick frying pan over high heat; pour about 2 tablespoons of batter into pan, tilting pan so batter coats base evenly. Cook, over low heat, loosening edge with spatula until crepe is browned lightly. Turn crepe; brown other side. Remove from pan; repeat with remaining batter to make 12 crepes.

4 Combine rind, juice, sugar, strained extra egg and butter in large heatproof bowl. Place bowl over large saucepan of simmering water; cook, stirring, about 15 minutes or until lemon curd coats the back of a spoon.

5 Sprinkle gelatine over the water in small heatproof jug. Stand jug in small saucepan of simmering water; stir until gelatine dissolves. Stir gelatine mixture into warm lemon curd.

6 Place one crepe in prepared pan; spread with ¹/₄ cup lemon curd. Continue layering with remaining crepes and curd, finishing with crepe layer. Cover; refrigerate overnight or until firm. Cut into wedges; top with crystallised rind (page 9), if desired.

SERVES 10

tip Simmering water should not touch the base of the heatproof bowl while making the lemon curd.

Tilt pan as soon as batter is added

Cook, stirring, until curd coats the spoon

Spread crepes with curd using a metal spatula

chocolate jaffa tart

PREPARATION TIME 30 MINUTES (plus refrigeration time)
COOKING TIME 55 MINUTES

1 Grease 24cm-round loose-based flan tin.

2 Blend or process flour, icing sugar and butter until crumbly.
   Add egg yolks and enough of the water to make ingredients just
   come together. Knead pastry on floured surface until smooth.
   Cover with plastic wrap; refrigerate 30 minutes.

3 Roll pastry, between sheets of baking paper, until large enough
   to line prepared tin; lift pastry into tin. Press into side; trim edge.
   Cover; refrigerate 30 minutes.

4 Preheat oven to moderately hot.

5 Cover pastry with baking paper; fill with dried beans or rice.
   Place on oven tray; bake in moderately hot oven 10 minutes.
   Remove paper and beans. Bake further 10 minutes or until pastry
   is browned lightly; cool.

6 Meanwhile, whisk eggs, rind, cream, caster sugar, chocolate, sifted
   cocoa powder and liqueur in medium bowl until combined.

7 Reduce oven temperature to moderate. Pour chocolate mixture
   into pastry case. Bake in moderate oven about 30 minutes or until
   filling is set; cool.

8 Place extra chocolate and extra cream in small saucepan; stir over
   low heat until smooth. Spread warm chocolate mixture over top of
   cold tart; refrigerate until set. Just before serving, decorate with
   Ferrero Rocher halves.

SERVES 8

tip Use a rolling pin to trim the edges of the pastry after it has been
eased into the tin; this makes a tidier cut than a knife.

1¹/₂ cups (225g) plain flour
¹/₄ cup (40g) icing sugar mixture
125g cold unsalted butter, chopped
2 egg yolks
2 teaspoons iced
water, approximately
3 eggs
1 tablespoon finely grated
orange rind
²/₃ cup (160ml) thickened cream
³/₄ cup (165g) caster sugar
60g dark chocolate, melted
2 tablespoons cocoa powder
2 tablespoons Grand Marnier
140g dark chocolate,
chopped coarsely, extra
¹/₄ cup (60ml) thickened
cream, extra
20 Ferrero Rocher
chocolates, halved

*hazelnuts and chocolate combine so well
in this luscious Ferrero Rocher treat*

chocolate nut bavarois with raspberry sauce

PREPARATION TIME 30 MINUTES (plus refrigeration time) • COOKING TIME 5 MINUTES

Nutella is a commercial spread made of milk chocolate and hazelnuts; it can be used in cooking, as here, or spread on your breakfast toast.

1 cup (250ml) milk
1/2 cup (165g) Nutella
4 egg yolks
1/4 cup (55g) caster sugar
2 teaspoons gelatine
1 tablespoon water
300ml thickened cream

RASPBERRY SAUCE

200g raspberries
2 tablespoons icing sugar mixture

1 Combine milk and Nutella in small saucepan. Stir over heat until Nutella melts; bring to a boil. Transfer to medium bowl.

2 Beat egg yolks and caster sugar in small bowl with electric mixer until thick and creamy; gradually stir into Nutella mixture.

3 Sprinkle gelatine over the water in small heatproof jug; stand in small saucepan of simmering water, stirring, until gelatine dissolves. Stir gelatine mixture into warm milk mixture; cool to room temperature.

4 Beat cream in small bowl with electric mixer until soft peaks form; fold into Nutella mixture. Divide bavarois mixture among six 3/4-cup (180ml) serving glasses; refrigerate about 4 hours. Top with raspberry sauce.

raspberry sauce Push raspberries through sieve into small bowl; discard seeds. Stir in sugar.

SERVES 6

tips If fresh raspberries are not available, you can use frozen raspberries, thawed, instead.
As a guide, when dissolved gelatine is added to a mixture, both should be roughly the same temperature.

raspberries, chocolate and hazelnuts are an unforgettable culinary trio

peanut butter and fudge ice-cream pie

PREPARATION TIME 20 MINUTES (plus refrigeration time)
COOKING TIME 10 MINUTES

1 Grease 24cm-round loose-based flan tin.

2 Blend or process cookies until mixture resembles coarse breadcrumbs. Add butter and milk; process until combined.

3 Using one hand, press cookie mixture evenly over base and around side of prepared tin; refrigerate 10 minutes.

4 Beat softened ice-cream and peanut butter in large bowl with electric mixer until combined. Spoon pie filling into crumb crust. Cover; freeze pie 3 hours or overnight.

5 Drizzle slices of pie with hot fudge sauce to serve.

hot fudge sauce Combine ingredients in small saucepan; stir over heat, without boiling, until smooth.

SERVES 10

tips Use a good quality ice-cream; various ice-creams differ from manufacturer to manufacturer, depending on the quantities of air and fat incorporated into the mixture.
Warm a large knife under hot water, quickly dry it and cut the pie while the knife is still hot.

300g packet chocolate
  chip cookies
40g butter, melted
1 tablespoon milk
1 litre vanilla ice-cream
1$^{1}/_{3}$ cups (375g) crunchy
  peanut butter

HOT FUDGE SAUCE

200g dark chocolate,
  chopped coarsely
50g white marshmallows,
  chopped coarsely
300ml thickened cream

marshmallows come in a variety of sizes and colours; the largest white type is best for this recipe

margarita mousse

PREPARATION TIME 20 MINUTES (plus refrigeration time) • COOKING TIME 5 MINUTES

*Although made with tequila and thought to be Mexican in origin,
the margarita was in fact invented in Texas for a poolside Christmas
party hosted by Margarita Sames, who named the drink after herself.
This recipe would have made the perfect dessert for that affair!*

1/4 cup (55g) white sugar
1 tablespoon gelatine
2 tablespoons water
1 cup (220g) caster sugar
1¼ cups (300g) sour cream
300ml thickened cream
1/2 cup (120g) spreadable
   cream cheese
green food colouring
1/4 cup (60ml) tequila
1 tablespoon Cointreau
1 teaspoon finely grated
   lime rind
3/4 cup (180ml) lime juice
1/3 cup (80ml) orange juice

1 Place white sugar on saucer. Dip rims of six 3/4-cup (180ml) glasses
   in bowl of cold water then into white sugar; refrigerate glasses.

2 Sprinkle gelatine over the water in small heatproof jug; stand jug in small
   saucepan of simmering water. Stir until gelatine dissolves; cool 5 minutes.

3 Beat caster sugar, sour cream, cream and cream cheese in medium bowl
   with electric mixer until sugar dissolves and mixture is fluffy. Beat in
   enough colouring to tint mixture a pale green.

4 Whisk tequila, liqueur, rind, juices and gelatine mixture into cream
   mixture. Divide mixture among prepared glasses; refrigerate about
   2 hours or until mousse sets.

SERVES 6

tips Mousse can be prepared a day ahead and refrigerated, covered,
until ready to serve.
Gelatine mixture should be cool but not set, and should be approximately
the same temperature as the cream mixture when they're combined;
if not, the mousse can split into layers or become somewhat rubbery.

*grate or zest only the green outer rind of
a lime to avoid the bitter white pith*

vanilla bean ice-cream with choc-almond crunch

PREPARATION TIME 20 MINUTES (plus refrigeration time)
COOKING TIME 20 MINUTES

1 Whisk egg yolks and sugar in medium bowl until light and fluffy.

2 Combine milk and cream in medium saucepan. Split vanilla bean in half lengthways; scrape seeds from bean. Add bean and seeds to pan; bring milk mixture almost to a boil.

3 Remove milk mixture from heat; discard vanilla bean. Whisking constantly, gradually pour milk mixture into egg mixture. Return custard mixture to same saucepan; cook over low heat, stirring constantly, until mixture begins to thicken and coats the back of a spoon (do not boil or mixture will curdle).

4 Return custard to same medium bowl. Cover surface completely with plastic wrap; freeze about 4 hours or until ice-cream is firm.

5 Line 8cm x 25cm bar cake pan with plastic wrap. Blend or process ice-cream until smooth; spread into prepared pan. Cover with foil; freeze until firm. Turn ice-cream out of pan; cut bar into 12 slices. Serve with shards of choc-almond crunch.

choc-almond crunch Combine sugar and the water in medium heavy-base saucepan; stir over low heat until sugar dissolves. Increase heat; bring to a boil. Boil, uncovered, without stirring, about 10 minutes or until syrup is a deep golden colour. Pour toffee mixture into 20cm x 30cm lamington pan; stand 5 minutes. Sprinkle chocolate over hot toffee, spreading with a palette knife to completely cover toffee. Sprinkle with almonds; refrigerate until set. Break choc-almond crunch into shards.

SERVES 6

tip Milk chocolate can be used instead of dark chocolate, if preferred.

2 egg yolks
1/3 cup (75g) caster sugar
1 cup (250ml) milk
300ml thickened cream
1 vanilla bean

CHOC-ALMOND CRUNCH

2 cups (440g) caster sugar
1 cup (250ml) water
200g dark chocolate, chopped coarsely
1/2 cup (40g) flaked almonds, toasted

Split vanilla bean lengthways

Scrape seeds out of vanilla bean

Spread chocolate evenly over hot toffee

fig and brioche pudding

PREPARATION TIME 15 MINUTES • COOKING TIME 1 HOUR 15 MINUTES

Brioche, a rich, slightly sweet yeast bread made with eggs and butter, is available at most bakeries.

1½ cups (375ml) milk

600ml cream

1 cinnamon stick

1 vanilla bean

¼ cup (90g) honey

4 eggs

2 small brioche (200g)

3 medium fresh figs (180g)

1 tablespoon demerara sugar

1 Stir milk, cream, cinnamon, vanilla bean and honey in medium saucepan until hot; strain into large heatproof jug.

2 Whisk eggs in large bowl; whisking constantly, pour hot milk mixture into egg mixture.

3 Preheat oven to moderate.

4 Cut each brioche into six slices and each fig into five slices. Layer brioche and figs, overlapping slightly, in lightly greased shallow 2-litre (8 cup) ovenproof dish. Pour hot milk mixture over brioche and figs; sprinkle with sugar.

5 Place pudding dish in large baking dish; add enough boiling water to come halfway up sides of dish; bake, uncovered, in moderate oven about 40 minutes or until pudding sets. Remove pudding dish from baking dish; stand 5 minutes before serving.

SERVES 6

tips Remove pudding from water bath immediately after cooking to prevent it from overcooking.
Whole vanilla bean can be rinsed under warm water, dried, then stored in an airtight jar for future use.
If you cannot find demerara sugar, use white sugar in its place.

fresh figs make a delicious treat when drizzled with honey then browned under a hot grill for a minute or two

raspberry and chocolate mousse trifle

PREPARATION TIME 30 MINUTES (plus refrigeration time)

Tia Maria, Kahlua and crème de caçao are all coffee-flavoured liqueurs; any one of them can be used in this recipe.

1 Combine chocolate and cream in small saucepan; stir over heat, without boiling, until smooth. Remove from heat; whisk in egg yolk. Transfer to medium bowl.

2 Place egg white and sugar in small bowl; beat with electric mixer until sugar dissolves. Gently fold egg white mixture into chocolate mixture. Cover; refrigerate mousse 3 hours or overnight.

3 Meanwhile, make jelly according to manufacturer's instructions; refrigerate until jelly just begins to set.

4 Cut sponge fingers into 1.5cm slices. Place slices over base and around side of deep 2-litre (8 cup) large serving bowl; drizzle evenly with liqueur. Pour jelly over sponge fingers; refrigerate until jelly sets.

5 Sprinkle half of the raspberries over jelly; spread evenly with mousse. Top with whipped extra cream and remaining raspberries. Sprinkle with chocolate shavings, if desired.

SERVES 6

tips Mousse can be prepared up to 2 days ahead; trifle can be assembled 1 day ahead.
If fresh raspberries are not available, frozen raspberries, thawed, can be substituted.
In step 3, jelly should set to the same consistency as an unbeaten egg white.

150g dark chocolate,
   chopped coarsely
1/2 cup (125ml) thickened cream
1 egg, separated
2 teaspoons caster sugar
85g packet raspberry jelly crystals
200g packaged chocolate sponge
   fingers (approximately 6)
1/4 cup (60ml) coffee-
   flavoured liqueur
1 cup (135g) raspberries
300ml thickened cream, extra

small cakes filled with mock cream are available in 200g packages at most supermarkets

flourless hazelnut chocolate cake

PREPARATION TIME 20 MINUTES (plus standing time) • COOKING TIME 1 HOUR

Hazelnut meal replaces the flour in this recipe.

¹/₃ cup (35g) cocoa powder
¹/₃ cup (80ml) hot water
150g dark chocolate, melted
150g butter, melted
1¹/₃ cups (275g) firmly packed
   brown sugar
1 cup (125g) hazelnut meal
4 eggs, separated
1 tablespoon cocoa powder, extra

1 Preheat oven to moderate. Grease deep 19cm-square cake pan; line base and sides with baking paper.

2 Blend cocoa with the hot water in large bowl until smooth. Stir in chocolate, butter, sugar, hazelnut meal and egg yolks.

3 Beat egg whites in small bowl with electric mixer until soft peaks form; fold into chocolate mixture in two batches.

4 Pour mixture into prepared pan; bake in moderate oven about 1 hour or until firm. Stand cake 15 minutes; turn onto wire rack, top-side up, to cool. Dust with sifted extra cocoa to serve.

SERVES 9

tip This cake can be made up to 4 days ahead and refrigerated, covered. It can also be frozen for up to 3 months.

hazelnut meal, also sold as ground hazelnuts, is a flour-like substance made after the nuts have been roasted

coco-cherry ice-cream timbale

PREPARATION TIME 10 MINUTES (plus refrigeration time)
COOKING TIME 2 MINUTES

Cherry Ripe is a chocolate bar filled with coconut and glacé cherries.

1 Soften ice-cream in large bowl; stir in Cherry Ripe, nuts, marshmallow, dark chocolate and enough colouring to tint the ice-cream pink. Divide mixture among eight 1-cup (250ml) moulds. Cover with foil; freeze 3 hours or overnight.

2 Place cream in small saucepan; bring to a boil. Remove from heat; add white chocolate. Stir until chocolate melts.

3 Turn ice-cream timbales onto serving plates; drizzle with warm white chocolate sauce.

SERVES 8

tip Use a good quality ice-cream; actual varieties of ice-cream differ from manufacturer to manufacturer depending on the quantities of air and fat incorporated into the mixture.

2 litres (8 cups) vanilla ice-cream
2 x 85g Cherry Ripe bars,
    chopped coarsely
1 cup (140g) vienna almonds,
    chopped coarsely
50g pink marshmallows,
    chopped coarsely
50g dark chocolate,
    chopped coarsely
pink food colouring
300ml cream
100g white chocolate,
    chopped finely

almonds coated in a toffee mixture are called vienna almonds; scorched almonds can be used instead

6 eggs

1 cup (220g) caster sugar

1/2 cup (75g) plain flour

1/2 cup (75g) self-raising flour

1/2 cup (75g) cornflour

1/4 cup (10g) instant
  coffee powder

1 1/2 cups (375ml) boiling water

3/4 cup (180ml) marsala

1/4 cup (60ml) coffee-
  flavoured liqueur

300ml thickened cream

1/2 cup (80g) icing sugar mixture

750g mascarpone cheese

500g vienna almonds,
  chopped coarsely

tiramisu torte

PREPARATION TIME 30 MINUTES • COOKING TIME 25 MINUTES

Tiramisu literally translated means "pick-me-up", and we have little doubt that this lusciously rich, cakey version will do just that. Vienna almonds are whole almonds that have been coated in a toffee mixture.

1 Preheat oven to moderate.

2 Grease two deep 22cm-round cake pans; line bases with baking paper.

3 Beat eggs in medium bowl with electric mixer about 10 minutes or until thick and creamy. Add caster sugar, about 1 tablespoon at a time, beating until sugar is dissolved between additions. Gently fold triple-sifted flours into egg mixture. Divide cake mixture evenly between prepared pans; bake in moderate oven about 25 minutes. Turn cakes, top-side up, onto wire racks to cool.

4 Meanwhile, dissolve coffee powder in the water in small heatproof bowl. Stir in marsala and liqueur; cool.

5 Beat cream and icing sugar in small bowl with electric mixer until soft peaks form; transfer to large bowl. Stir in mascarpone and 1/2 cup of the coffee mixture.

6 Split cooled cakes in half. Centre half of one cake on serving plate; brush with a quarter of the remaining coffee mixture then spread with about 1 cup of mascarpone cream. Repeat layering until last cake half is covered with mascarpone cream. Spread remaining mascarpone cream around side of cake; press almonds into side and top of cake. Refrigerate until ready to serve.

SERVES 12

tip This cake is best made a day ahead and kept, refrigerated, in an airtight container.

Brush coffee mixture onto top of each cake

Spread mascarpone cream around cake

Press vienna almonds into mascarpone cream

lemon curd cheesecake

PREPARATION TIME 30 MINUTES (plus standing time)
COOKING TIME 1 HOUR

What a great combo – the tang of lemon curd and the creaminess of baked cheesecake. We used a 250g packet of Nice biscuits for this recipe.

1 Blend or process biscuits until mixture resembles fine breadcrumbs. Add butter; process until just combined. Using one hand, press biscuit mixture evenly over base and side of 22cm springform tin. Cover; refrigerate 30 minutes or until firm.

2 Meanwhile, preheat oven to moderate. Beat cheese, sugar and rind in large bowl with electric mixer until smooth; beat in eggs, one at a time.

3 Place tin on oven tray; pour cheesecake mixture into tin. Bake in moderate oven about 1 hour or until set. Remove from oven; cool in tin to room temperature.

4 Spread top of cheesecake with lemon curd; refrigerate 3 hours or overnight. Remove from tin just before serving.

lemon curd Combine ingredients in medium heatproof bowl. Place bowl over medium saucepan of simmering water; cook, stirring constantly, about 20 minutes or until mixture coats the back of a spoon. Remove bowl from saucepan immediately to avoid further cooking; cool to room temperature.

SERVES 10

tip It's important that the base of the bowl containing the lemon curd does not touch the simmering water.

250g plain sweet biscuits
125g butter, melted
3 x 250g packets cream
 cheese, softened
1/2 cup (110g) caster sugar
2 teaspoons finely grated
 lemon rind
3 eggs

LEMON CURD

45g butter
1/2 cup (110g) caster sugar
1 egg, beaten lightly, strained
1 teaspoon finely grated
 lemon rind
2 tablespoons lemon juice

plain un-iced sweet biscuits produce the perfect texture for a cheesecake crust, having an almost nut-like crunch

lemon bombes alaska

PREPARATION TIME 40 MINUTES (plus refrigeration time)
COOKING TIME 20 MINUTES

2³/₄ cups (680ml) slightly
softened vanilla ice-cream
30g unsalted butter
¹/₂ teaspoon finely grated
lemon rind
1 tablespoon lemon juice
1 egg yolk
¹/₄ cup (55g) caster sugar
¹/₃ cup (80ml) limoncello
¹/₂ cup (125ml) thickened cream
290g packet sponge cake
2 egg whites
¹/₃ cup (75g) caster sugar, extra

1 Line four ¹/₂-cup (125ml) moulds with plastic wrap. Press ¹/₃ cup ice-cream firmly up and around inside of each mould to form cavity. Cover with foil; freeze 2 hours. Return remaining ice-cream to freezer.

2 Combine butter, rind, juice, egg yolk and sugar in small heatproof bowl; stir over small saucepan of simmering water until mixture thickens slightly. Stir in liqueur. Cover surface of lemon curd with plastic wrap; refrigerate until cold.

3 Place 1 tablespoon of the lemon curd into each mould, cover; freeze until firm. Combine remaining lemon curd with cream, cover; refrigerate lemon cream until serving.

4 Remove moulds from the freezer, spread enough remaining ice-cream over lemon curd to fill moulds; cover, freeze bombes until firm.

5 Preheat oven to very hot.

6 Cut four rounds from sponge cake, large enough to cover top of each mould.

7 Beat egg whites in small bowl with electric mixer until soft peaks form; add extra sugar, 1 tablespoon at a time, beating until sugar dissolves between additions.

8 Turn one bombe onto one round of sponge cake on oven tray; peel away plastic wrap. Spread a quarter of the meringue mixture over to enclose bombe completely; repeat with remaining bombes, sponge and meringue mixture. Bake bombes, uncovered, in very hot oven about 3 minutes or until browned lightly. Serve immediately with lemon cream.

SERVES 4

tip Bombes can be prepared the day before serving to the stage at which they are ready to be baked; store in the freezer.

Press ice-cream around inside of moulds

Spoon then spread ice-cream over lemon curd

Spread meringue all over each bombe

mars bar cheesecake

PREPARATION TIME 30 MINUTES (plus refrigeration time)
COOKING TIME 5 MINUTES

1 Blend or process biscuits until mixture resembles fine breadcrumbs. Add butter; process until just combined. Using one hand, press biscuit mixture evenly over base and side of 20cm springform tin, cover; refrigerate about 30 minutes or until firm.

2 Meanwhile, combine brown sugar, extra butter and 2 tablespoons of the cream in small saucepan; stir over low heat, until sugar dissolves, to make butterscotch sauce.

3 Combine chocolate and another 2 tablespoons of the cream in another small saucepan; stir over low heat until chocolate melts.

4 Sprinkle gelatine over the water in small heatproof jug; stand jug in small saucepan of simmering water. Stir until gelatine dissolves; cool 5 minutes.

5 Beat cheese and caster sugar in medium bowl with electric mixer until smooth. Beat remaining cream in small bowl with electric mixer until soft peaks form. Stir slightly warm gelatine mixture into cheese mixture with Mars bars; fold in cream.

6 Pour half of the cheese mixture into prepared tin; drizzle half of the butterscotch and chocolate sauces over cheese mixture. Pull skewer backwards and forwards through mixture several times to create marbled effect. Repeat process with remaining cheese mixture and sauces. Cover cheesecake; refrigerate about 3 hours or until set.

SERVES 8

tips Because of the long refrigeration time, this recipe is a good one to prepare a day ahead if you're entertaining.
You can also melt the milk chocolate and cream in a microwave oven; cook on HIGH (100%) about 1 minute, stirring twice while cooking.

250g plain chocolate biscuits
150g butter, melted
2 tablespoons brown sugar
20g butter, extra
300ml thickened cream
50g milk chocolate,
   chopped finely
3 teaspoons gelatine
1/4 cup (60ml) water
2 x 250g packets cream
   cheese, softened
1/2 cup (110g) caster sugar
3 x 60g Mars bars, chopped finely

kept in the fridge or freezer, Mars bars can be chopped and sprinkled over ice-cream for a quick dessert

cakes

cherry-ripe mud cake

PREPARATION TIME 35 MINUTES (plus standing time) • COOKING TIME 2 HOURS

250g unsalted butter, chopped

1 tablespoon instant
   coffee powder

1²/₃ cups (400ml) coconut milk

200g dark chocolate,
   chopped coarsely

2 cups (440g) caster sugar

³/₄ cup (110g) self-raising flour

1 cup (150g) plain flour

¹/₄ cup (25g) cocoa powder

2 eggs

2 teaspoons vanilla essence

2 x 85g Cherry Ripe bars,
   chopped coarsely

200g dark chocolate,
   chopped coarsely, extra

125g unsalted butter,
   chopped, extra

CHOCOLATE PANELS

300g dark chocolate Melts

1 teaspoon vegetable oil

1 Preheat oven to slow. Grease deep 22cm-round cake pan; line base and side with baking paper.

2 Melt butter in large saucepan; add coffee, coconut milk, chocolate and sugar. Stir over heat until chocolate melts and sugar dissolves; cool to room temperature.

3 Whisk in sifted dry ingredients, then eggs and essence; stir in half of the Cherry Ripe. Pour mixture into prepared pan. Top with remaining Cherry Ripe; bake in slow oven about 1³/₄ hours. Stand cake 10 minutes; turn, top-side up, onto wire rack to cool.

4 Combine extra chocolate and extra butter in small saucepan; stir over low heat until smooth. Refrigerate until mixture is of spreadable consistency.

5 Spread chocolate mixture all over cake; place chocolate panels around side of cake. Serve with whipped cream, if desired.

chocolate panels Combine chocolate and oil in medium heatproof bowl; stir over medium saucepan of simmering water until smooth. Cut two 6cm x 50cm strips of baking paper. Spread chocolate evenly over strips; lift strips to allow chocolate to drip off paper. Allow chocolate to set, then, using ruler as guide, cut chocolate into 4cm panels with sharp knife. Carefully peel away baking paper.

SERVES 12

tip You can also melt the chocolate for the chocolate panels in a microwave oven; cook on MEDIUM (55%) about 1 minute, stirring twice during cooking. Stir in the oil once the chocolate has melted.

Spread chocolate onto baking paper strips

Allow excess chocolate to drip from paper

Position panels around side of cake

mixed berry cake with vanilla bean syrup

PREPARATION TIME 20 MINUTES • COOKING TIME 40 MINUTES

Vanilla beans – the dried, thin pods of a tropical orchid grown in Tahiti, Madagascar and Central and South America – should be kept in an airtight container in a cool, dark place.

1 Preheat oven to moderate. Grease 20cm baba pan thoroughly.

2 Beat butter and sugar in small bowl with electric mixer until light and fluffy. Add eggs, one at a time, beating until just combined between additions. Mixture may curdle at this stage but will come together later.

3 Transfer mixture to large bowl; stir in sifted flours, almond meal, sour cream, berries and cherries. Pour mixture into prepared pan; bake, uncovered, in moderate oven about 40 minutes. Stand cake 5 minutes; turn onto wire rack placed over a large tray. Pour hot vanilla bean syrup over hot cake.

vanilla bean syrup Combine the water and sugar in small saucepan. Split vanilla beans in half lengthways; scrape seeds into pan then place pods in pan. Stir over heat, without boiling, until sugar dissolves. Simmer, uncovered, without stirring, 5 minutes. Using tongs, remove pods from syrup.

SERVES 8

125g butter, chopped
1 cup (220g) caster sugar
3 eggs
1/2 cup (75g) plain flour
1/4 cup (35g) self-raising flour
1/2 cup (60g) almond meal
1/3 cup (80g) sour cream
1 1/2 cups (225g) frozen
    mixed berries
1/2 cup (100g) drained canned
    seeded black cherries

VANILLA BEAN SYRUP
1/2 cup (125ml) water
1/2 cup (110g) caster sugar
2 vanilla beans

vanilla beans contain a myriad tiny black seeds which impart their full flavour to both sweet and savoury dishes

double-decker mud cake

PREPARATION TIME 30 MINUTES (plus standing time) • COOKING TIME 1 HOUR

250g butter, chopped

150g white chocolate,
    chopped coarsely

2 cups (440g) caster sugar

1 cup (250ml) milk

1¹/2 cups (225g) plain flour

¹/2 cup (75g) self-raising flour

1 teaspoon vanilla essence

2 eggs, beaten lightly

2 tablespoons cocoa powder

600g milk chocolate,
    chopped coarsely

1 cup (250ml) cream

1 Preheat oven to slow. Grease two deep 20cm-round cake pans; line
   bases and sides with baking paper.

2 Combine butter, white chocolate, sugar and milk in medium saucepan;
   stir over heat, without boiling, until smooth. Transfer mixture to large
   bowl; cool 15 minutes.

3 Whisk sifted flours into white chocolate mixture then whisk in essence
   and egg; pour half of the mixture into one of the prepared pans. Whisk
   sifted cocoa into remaining mixture; pour into other prepared pan.
   Bake cakes in slow oven about 50 minutes. Stand cakes 5 minutes;
   turn cakes, top-side up, onto wire rack to cool.

4 Combine milk chocolate and cream in medium saucepan; stir over low
   heat until smooth. Transfer to medium bowl. Cover; refrigerate, stirring
   occasionally, until chocolate mixture is of spreadable consistency.
   Reserve 1 cup of the chocolate mixture for spreading over cake.

5 Split each cooled cake in half. Centre one layer of cake on serving
   plate; spread with ¹/2 cup of the remaining milk chocolate mixture.
   Repeat layering, alternating colours. Cover top and sides of cake with
   reserved chocolate mixture.

SERVES 10

tip You can also melt the milk chocolate and cream in a microwave
oven; cook on HIGH (100%) about 1¹/2 minutes, pausing to stir
every 30 seconds.

*butter can be softened by placing it, in
a microwave-safe bowl, in your microwave
oven on HIGH, for about 10 seconds*

irish cream and dark chocolate mousse cake

PREPARATION TIME 30 MINUTES (plus refrigeration time)
COOKING TIME 15 MINUTES

We used Baileys Irish Cream in this recipe – a liqueur made of a blend of cream, Irish whiskey and Irish spirits.

1 Preheat oven to moderate. Grease 25cm x 30cm swiss roll pan; line base and sides with baking paper.

2 Beat egg yolks and sugar in small bowl with electric mixer until thick and creamy; transfer to large bowl. Fold in combined sifted cocoa and cornflour, then chocolate; fold in the water.

3 Beat egg whites in medium bowl with electric mixer until soft peaks form. Fold egg whites, in two batches, into chocolate mixture. Spread mixture into prepared pan; bake in moderate oven about 15 minutes. Turn cake onto baking-paper-covered wire rack. Cover cake with baking paper; cool to room temperature.

4 Grease 22cm springform tin; line side with baking paper, bringing paper 5cm above edge of tin. Cut 22cm-diameter circle from cooled cake; place in prepared tin. Discard remaining cake.

5 Combine cream and extra chocolate in medium saucepan; stir over low heat until smooth. Transfer to large bowl; refrigerate until just cold.

6 Add liqueur to chocolate mixture; beat with electric mixer until mixture changes to a paler colour. Pour mixture into prepared tin; refrigerate about 3 hours or until set.

7 Transfer cake from tin to serving plate; dust with sifted extra cocoa.

SERVES 12

tip Do not overbeat the chocolate and liqueur mixture as it will curdle.

6 eggs, separated
1/2 cup (80g) icing sugar mixture
1/4 cup (25g) cocoa powder
2 tablespoons cornflour
150g dark chocolate, melted
1 tablespoon water
600ml thickened cream
450g dark chocolate,
  chopped coarsely, extra
3/4 cup (180ml) irish
  cream liqueur
1 tablespoon cocoa powder, extra

Beat the eggs yolks until light and creamy

Fold beaten egg white into chocolate mixture

Cut a 22cm-circle out of cake

chocolate butterscotch cake

PREPARATION TIME 20 MINUTES (plus refrigeration time) • COOKING TIME 1 HOUR

1/4 cup (25g) cocoa powder
250g butter, softened
1 cup (200g) firmly packed
    dark brown sugar
2 eggs
1 tablespoon golden syrup
1¹/4 cups (185g) self-raising flour
1/2 cup (125ml) milk

MASCARPONE CREAM

250g mascarpone cheese
300ml thickened cream

CARAMEL ICING

60g butter
1/2 cup (100g) firmly packed
    dark brown sugar
1/4 cup (60ml) milk
1¹/2 cups (240g) icing
    sugar mixture

1 Preheat oven to moderate. Grease deep 20cm-round cake pan;
line base and side with baking paper.

2 Sift cocoa into large bowl; add remaining ingredients. Beat with
electric mixer on low speed until combined. Increase speed to medium;
beat until mixture has just changed in colour. Pour mixture into
prepared pan; bake in moderate oven about 1 hour. Stand cake
10 minutes; turn, top-side up, onto wire rack to cool.

3 Using large serrated knife, split cake into three layers. Centre one layer
on serving plate; spread with a third of the mascarpone cream and a
third of the caramel icing. Repeat with second layer and half of the
remaining mascarpone cream and half of the remaining caramel icing;
top with remaining cake layer. Cover top cake layer with remaining
mascarpone cream then drizzle with remaining caramel icing. Swirl for
marbled effect; refrigerate about 30 minutes or until icing is firm.

mascarpone cream Whisk mascarpone and cream in small bowl until
soft peaks form.

caramel icing Heat butter, brown sugar and milk in small saucepan,
stirring constantly, without boiling, until sugar dissolves; remove from
heat. Add icing sugar; stir until smooth.

SERVES 10

tip Do not overbeat the mascarpone cream mixture as it could curdle.

*mascarpone, a creamy, soft, extremely
rich Italian cheese, is delicious simply
served on its own with a platter of fruit*

maple pecan cake

PREPARATION TIME 15 MINUTES • COOKING TIME 1 HOUR

1 Preheat oven to moderate. Grease deep 20cm-round cake pan;
line base with baking paper. Spray paper with oil.

2 Arrange nuts over base of prepared pan; drizzle with maple syrup.

3 Combine the water, figs and soda in bowl of food processor.
Cover with lid; stand 5 minutes. Add butter and sugar; process
until almost smooth. Add eggs and flour; process until just combined.
Pour mixture into prepared pan; bake in moderate oven about
55 minutes. Stand cake 5 minutes; turn onto wire rack. Serve with
maple butterscotch sauce and, if desired, vanilla ice-cream.

maple butterscotch sauce Stir ingredients in small saucepan over
heat until smooth; bring to a boil. Boil, uncovered, about 2 minutes
or until mixture thickens slightly.

SERVES 10

tip Either maple syrup or maple-flavoured syrup can be
used in this recipe.

cooking-oil spray
1 cup (100g) pecans
1/3 cup (80ml) maple syrup
1¼ cups (310ml) boiling water
1¼ cups (235g) coarsely
 chopped dried figs
1 teaspoon bicarbonate of soda
60g butter
3/4 cup (150g) firmly
 packed brown sugar
2 eggs
1 cup (150g) self-raising flour

MAPLE BUTTERSCOTCH SAUCE
1 cup (250ml) maple syrup
1/2 cup (125ml) cream
100g butter, chopped

*maple syrup, made from the refined sap
of the North American maple tree, is dark
amber in colour and very thick*

125g unsalted butter, chopped

2 teaspoons instant coffee powder

3/4 cup (180ml) water

100g dark chocolate,
chopped coarsely

1 cup (220g) caster sugar

1 egg, beaten lightly

3/4 cup (110g) self-raising flour

1/2 cup (75g) plain flour

2 tablespoons cocoa powder

PEPPERMINT CREAM

125g unsalted butter, chopped

3 cups (480g) icing sugar mixture

2 tablespoons milk

1/2 teaspoon peppermint essence

green food colouring

CHOCOLATE GANACHE

300g dark chocolate,
chopped coarsely

1 cup (250ml) cream

chocolate peppermint cake

PREPARATION TIME 20 MINUTES (plus refrigeration time) • COOKING TIME 1 HOUR

1 Preheat oven to slow. Grease two 8cm x 25cm bar cake pans;
line bases and sides with baking paper.

2 Stir butter, coffee, the water, chocolate and sugar in medium saucepan
over heat until smooth. Transfer mixture to medium bowl. Whisk in
egg with sifted flours and cocoa. Pour mixture equally between
prepared pans; bake in slow oven about 45 minutes. Stand cakes
5 minutes; turn, top-side up, onto wire rack to cool.

3 Using serrated knife, split cooled cakes in half. Place bottom layers
on wire rack over tray. Spread each with about a quarter of the
peppermint cream; top with cake tops. Place remaining peppermint
cream in piping bag fitted with 2cm fluted tube. Pipe remaining
cream along centre of each cake top; refrigerate 1 hour.

4 Using metal spatula and working quickly, pour chocolate ganache over
cakes, smoothing sides. Stand at room temperature until ganache sets.

peppermint cream Beat butter in small bowl with electric mixer
until as pale as possible. Gradually beat in icing sugar, milk, essence
and enough of the colouring to tint to the desired shade of green.

chocolate ganache Combine chocolate and cream in small saucepan;
stir over low heat until smooth.

SERVES 20

tip The butter for both the cakes and the peppermint cream should
be at room temperature before beating.

Beat peppermint cream until light and fluffy

Pipe peppermint cream onto cakes

Pour ganache over cakes

whole tangelo cake

PREPARATION TIME 20 MINUTES • COOKING TIME 45 MINUTES

*Tangelos are a cross between a grapefruit and a tangerine, tasting more like
the latter but closer in size to the former. You need four tangelos for this recipe.*

1 Place tangelos in medium saucepan; cover with cold water. Bring to a
boil; drain. Repeat process two more times; cool to room temperature.

2 Preheat oven to moderate. Grease deep 22cm-round cake pan; line base
and side with baking paper.

3 Halve tangelos; discard seeds. Blend or process tangelo until pulpy;
transfer to large bowl.

4 Beat butter, sugar and eggs together in small bowl with electric
mixer until light and fluffy. Add creamed mixture to tangelo pulp;
stir until combined.

5 Stir in sifted flours with coconut; pour mixture into prepared pan.
Bake in moderate oven about 45 minutes. Stand cake 5 minutes;
turn, top-side up, onto wire rack over tray. Pour hot tangelo syrup
over hot cake. Return any syrup that drips onto tray into jug; pour
over cake. Serve cake warm.

tangelo syrup Using wooden spoon, stir ingredients in small
saucepan over heat, without boiling, until sugar dissolves; bring to
a boil. Reduce heat; simmer, uncovered, without stirring, 2 minutes.
Pour into medium heatproof jug.

SERVES 16

tips The cake, with or without syrup, can be stored in an airtight
container for up to 2 days. Without syrup, the cake can be frozen
for up to 3 months.
Any citrus fruit can be substituted for the tangelo, and cake can be
topped with crystallised rind (page 9).

2 medium tangelos (420g)
125g butter, chopped
1¹/₂ cups (330g) caster sugar
2 eggs
1 cup (150g) self-raising flour
¹/₂ cup (75g) plain flour
¹/₂ cup (45g) desiccated coconut

TANGELO SYRUP

1 cup (220g) caster sugar
rind of 1 tangelo, sliced thinly
²/₃ cup (160ml) tangelo juice
¹/₃ cup (80ml) water

*desiccated coconut, the crisp, finely
shredded, dried meat of the coconut, is
used both in baking and cake decorating*

pistachio and hazelnut friends with toffee shards

PREPARATION TIME 20 MINUTES • COOKING TIME 30 MINUTES

Rosewater is an extract made from crushed rose petals, called gulab in India. It's used in many sweets and desserts for its aromatic quality.

6 egg whites

185g butter, melted

3/4 cup (75g) hazelnut meal

1/4 cup (35g) roasted shelled
   pistachios, chopped coarsely

11/2 cups (240g) icing
   sugar mixture

1/2 cup (75g) plain flour

2 teaspoons rosewater

1/3 cup (50g) roasted shelled
   pistachios, extra

TOFFEE SHARDS

2/3 cup (160ml) water

11/3 cups (300g) caster sugar

1 Preheat oven to moderately hot. Grease eight 1/2-cup (125ml) oval or rectangular friand pans; stand on oven tray.

2 Place egg whites in medium bowl; whisk lightly with fork until combined. Add butter, hazelnut meal, nuts, sugar, flour and rosewater; using wooden spoon, stir until just combined.

3 Pour mixture equally among prepared pans; top with extra nuts. Bake in moderately hot oven about 30 minutes. Stand friands 5 minutes; turn, top-side up, onto wire rack. Serve friands warm or at room temperature with toffee shards and thick cream, if desired.

toffee shards Using wooden spoon, stir ingredients in small saucepan over heat, without boiling, until sugar dissolves; bring to a boil. Reduce heat; simmer, uncovered, without stirring, about 10 minutes or until toffee is golden brown. Remove from heat; allow bubbles to subside. Pour hot toffee onto lightly oiled oven tray; do not scrape the toffee from pan, or it might crystallise. Allow toffee to set at room temperature; break into shards with hands.

SERVES 8

tip You can use frozen egg whites, thawed, in this recipe. These are readily available in supermarkets.

pistachios marry especially well with rosewater, as seen here and in several of the different varieties of baklava

berry-mousse cake

PREPARATION TIME 40 MINUTES (plus refrigeration time)
COOKING TIME 20 MINUTES

Malibu is a liqueur made from rum and coconut. If you don't like the taste of coconut, substitute plain white rum for Malibu in this recipe.

1 Preheat oven to moderate. Grease two 22cm springform tins; line bases with baking paper.

2 Beat egg whites in medium bowl with electric mixer until soft peaks form. Gradually add sugar, beating between additions, until sugar dissolves; fold in dry ingredients.

3 Spread mixture equally between prepared tins; bake in moderate oven about 20 minutes. Stand cakes 5 minutes. Remove from tins; cool at room temperature.

4 Line base and side of clean 22cm springform tin with baking paper; return one cake to tin. Pour raspberry mousse over cake; top with remaining cake. Cover; refrigerate 3 hours or overnight, until mousse sets.

5 Remove cake from tin. Beat cream in small bowl with electric mixer until soft peaks form; spread all over cake. Place raspberries on top of cake; brush raspberries with combined strained jam and liqueur.

raspberry mousse Push raspberries through sieve into large bowl; discard seeds. Sprinkle gelatine over the water in small heatproof jug. Stand jug in small saucepan of simmering water; stir until gelatine dissolves. Combine gelatine mixture, chocolate, egg yolks, sugar and liqueur in small bowl; stir until smooth. Beat cream in small bowl with electric mixer until soft peaks form; fold cream and chocolate mixture into raspberry puree.

SERVES 12

tips Prepare the raspberry mousse while cake is baking.
The cake, without the topping, can be made a day ahead.

4 egg whites
3/4 cup (165g) caster sugar
11/2 cups (240g) almond meal
1/4 cup (35g) plain flour
300ml thickened cream
450g fresh raspberries
1/2 cup (160g) raspberry
   jam, warmed
1/4 cup (60ml) Malibu

RASPBERRY MOUSSE

200g fresh raspberries
3 teaspoons gelatine
2 tablespoons water
125g white chocolate, melted
2 egg yolks
1/4 cup (55g) caster sugar
1 tablespoon Malibu
300ml thickened cream

Push raspberries through sieve into bowl

Combine mousse ingredients carefully

Place top cake layer over mousse in pan

chocolate cappuccino cakes

PREPARATION TIME 30 MINUTES • COOKING TIME 25 MINUTES

Tia Maria, Kahlua and crème de caçao are all coffee-flavoured liqueurs; any one of them can be used in this recipe.

1 tablespoon instant
   coffee powder
¹/₄ cup (60ml) hot water
4 eggs
¹/₄ cup (50g) firmly packed
   brown sugar
400g dark chocolate, melted
¹/₂ cup (120g) sour cream
¹/₂ cup (75g) self-raising flour
¹/₄ cup (60ml) coffee-
   flavoured liqueur
1 cup (150g) dark chocolate
   Melts, melted
1²/₃ cups (400ml)
   thickened cream
1 tablespoon icing sugar mixture
2 tablespoons coffee-flavoured
   liqueur, extra
2 teaspoons cocoa powder
24 chocolate-coated
   coffee beans (50g)

1 Preheat oven to moderate. Grease 20cm x 30cm lamington pan; line base and sides with baking paper.

2 Dissolve coffee in the water in small jug; cool. Beat eggs and brown sugar in small bowl with electric mixer until thick and pale; transfer mixture to large bowl. Fold coffee mixture, dark chocolate, sour cream and flour into egg mixture.

3 Spread cake mixture into prepared pan; bake in moderate oven 25 minutes. Cool cake in pan; turn cake onto board. Cut eight rounds from cake using 7cm cutter; brush rounds with liqueur on one side.

4 Cut eight 12cm x 24cm strips of baking paper. Fold each strip in half lengthways; fold one short edge over by 1cm to make a "handle" to hold when paper is eventually removed from chocolate. Lay one strip on large piece of baking paper; using metal spatula, spread strip evenly with chocolate Melts. Lift chocolate strip off baking paper; wrap around one cake round, leaving strip's folded edge at cake base and "handle" facing out. Repeat with remaining strips, chocolate Melts and cake rounds. Stand at room temperature until chocolate sets then, using "handle", carefully remove baking paper.

5 Whip cream and icing sugar in small bowl with electric mixer until soft peaks form; fold in extra liqueur. Spoon cream mixture onto chocolate cakes; dust with sifted cocoa. Top with chocolate coated coffee beans.

SERVES 8

tip Chocolate cappuccino cases can be prepared a day ahead and covered, at room temperature, until ready to fill with coffee cream.

Spread baking paper strip with chocolate

Wrap one chocolate strip around each cake

Use handle to remove paper strip

pear and almond cake with passionfruit glaze

PREPARATION TIME 30 MINUTES • COOKING TIME 50 MINUTES

You will need about four passionfruit for this recipe.

1 Preheat oven to moderately slow. Grease 22cm springform tin; line base and side with baking paper.

2 Beat butter and sugar in medium bowl with electric mixer until light and fluffy. Add eggs, one at a time, beating until combined between each addition. Stir in almond meal and flour.

3 Spread mixture into prepared pan; top with pear halves. Bake in moderately slow oven about 50 minutes; stand cake 5 minutes. Remove from pan; turn, top-side up, onto wire rack. Pour passionfruit glaze over cake.

passionfruit glaze Stir combined ingredients in small saucepan over heat, without boiling, until sugar dissolves. Bring to a boil; reduce heat. Simmer, uncovered, without stirring, about 2 minutes or until thickened slightly; cool.

SERVES 10

tip Cake and glaze can be made a day ahead and refrigerated, covered separately, until required.

185g butter, chopped
1/2 cup (110g) caster sugar
3 eggs
11/2 cups (185g) almond meal
1/4 cup (35g) plain flour
420g can pear halves in natural juice, drained

PASSIONFRUIT GLAZE

1/3 cup (80ml) passionfruit pulp
1/3 cup (80ml) light corn syrup
1 tablespoon caster sugar

canned pears generally hold their shape well when used in baking, and don't lose any of their sweet, juicy flavour

warm apple cake with brandy butterscotch sauce

PREPARATION TIME 30 MINUTES • COOKING TIME 40 MINUTES

125g butter, chopped

1/2 cup (110g) caster sugar

2 eggs

2/3 cup (100g) self-raising flour

1/3 cup (50g) plain flour

1 tablespoon milk

3 medium granny smith
    apples (450g)

1/2 cup (160g) apricot
    jam, warmed

BRANDY BUTTERSCOTCH SAUCE

1/2 cup (100g) firmly packed
    brown sugar

1/2 cup (125ml) thickened cream

100g butter, chopped

2 tablespoons brandy

1 Preheat oven to moderately slow. Grease and line base and sides of two 8cm x 25cm bar cake pans.

2 Beat butter and sugar in small bowl with electric mixer until light and fluffy. Beat in eggs, one at a time, beating until combined between each addition. Stir in sifted flours and milk; spread mixture into prepared pans.

3 Peel, core and halve apples; slice halves thinly. Push apple slices gently into surface of cake mixture.

4 Brush apple with strained jam; bake cakes in moderately slow oven about 40 minutes. Stand cakes 10 minutes; turn, top-side up, onto wire rack to cool. Serve pieces of cake warm, drizzled with brandy butterscotch sauce.

brandy butterscotch sauce Combine ingredients in small saucepan. Stir over heat, without boiling, until sugar dissolves; bring to a boil. Reduce heat; simmer, uncovered, without stirring, about 3 minutes or until mixture thickens slightly.

SERVES 8

tip Peel, core and cut apples just before using to prevent the flesh browning.

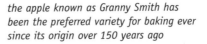

the apple known as Granny Smith has been the preferred variety for baking ever since its origin over 150 years ago

chocolate fruit cake

PREPARATION TIME 20 MINUTES • COOKING TIME 1 HOUR

1 Preheat oven to slow. Grease 20cm-ring pan; line base with baking paper.

2 Combine butter, sugar, chocolate and the water in medium saucepan; stir over heat until sugar dissolves. Remove from heat; stir in rum, nuts and fruit. Add sifted dry ingredients and egg; stir until combined.

3 Spoon mixture into prepared pan; bake in slow oven about 1 hour. Cool cake in pan.

4 Just before serving, combine cooled extra chocolate and sour cream in small bowl; stir until smooth. Turn cake onto serving plate, top-side up; spread chocolate mixture over top of cake.

SERVES 12

tip The chocolate fruit cake can be baked in a 14cm x 21cm loaf pan; bake in a slow oven about 1½ hours.

125g butter, chopped
3/4 cup (150g) firmly packed
   brown sugar
50g dark chocolate,
   chopped coarsely
1/2 cup (125ml) water
1/4 cup (60ml) dark rum
1/4 cup (30g) coarsely
   chopped walnuts
1/2 cup (75g) dried currants
1 cup (160g) sultanas
1 cup (170g) coarsely
   chopped raisins
1/4 cup (40g) mixed peel
3/4 cup (110g) plain flour
2 tablespoons cocoa powder
2 tablespoons self-raising flour
1/2 teaspoon mixed spice
2 eggs, beaten lightly
80g dark chocolate, melted, extra
1/4 cup (60g) sour cream

walnuts marry well with apple and can be used in savoury as well as sweet dishes

chocolate roulade with coffee cream

PREPARATION TIME 20 MINUTES • COOKING TIME 10 MINUTES

Tia Maria, Kahlua and crème de caçao are all coffee-flavoured liqueurs; any one of them can be used in this recipe.

1 tablespoon caster sugar

200g dark chocolate,
   chopped coarsely

1/4 cup (60ml) hot water

1 tablespoon instant
   coffee powder

4 eggs, separated

1/2 cup (110g) caster sugar, extra

1 teaspoon hot water, extra

300ml thickened cream

2 tablespoons coffee-
   flavoured liqueur

1 tablespoon icing sugar mixture

1 Preheat oven to moderate. Grease 25cm x 30cm swiss roll pan; line base with baking paper. Place a piece of baking paper cut the same size as swiss roll pan on board or bench; sprinkle evenly with caster sugar.

2 Combine chocolate, the water and half of the coffee powder in large heatproof bowl. Stir over large saucepan of simmering water until smooth; remove from heat.

3 Beat egg yolks and extra caster sugar in small bowl with electric mixer until thick and creamy; fold egg mixture into warm chocolate mixture.

4 Meanwhile, beat egg whites in small bowl with electric mixer until soft peaks form; fold egg whites, in two batches, into chocolate mixture. Spread into prepared pan; bake in moderate oven about 10 minutes.

5 Turn cake onto sugared paper, peeling baking paper away; use serrated knife to cut away crisp edges from all sides. Cover cake with tea towel; cool.

6 Dissolve remaining coffee powder in the extra water in small bowl. Add cream, liqueur and icing sugar; beat with electric mixer until firm peaks form. Spread cake evenly with cream mixture. Roll cake, from long side, by lifting paper and using it to guide the roll into shape. Cover roll; refrigerate 30 minutes before serving.

SERVES 8

tip Be sure you beat the egg yolk mixture until thick, and the egg whites only until soft peaks form. Overbeating will dry out the egg whites and make them difficult to fold into the chocolate mixture.

Fold egg whites into chocolate mixture

Turn cake onto sugared paper

Use the sugared paper to help roll cake

light and dark fruit cake

PREPARATION TIME 30 MINUTES (plus standing time) • COOKING TIME 2 HOURS

Marzipan, a pliable paste made from ground blanched almonds, sugar and egg whites, is used to shape and mould different decorations for cakes and pastries and can be found at your local supermarket.

1 Combine fruit and rum in medium bowl, cover; stand overnight.

2 Line 20cm x 30cm lamington pan with baking paper, extending paper 3cm over long sides of pan.

3 Beat butter, sugar and eggs in small bowl with electric mixer until light and fluffy. Mixture may curdle at this point but will come together later.

4 Add butter mixture to fruit mixture; stir in nuts, chocolate and sifted dry ingredients. Spread mixture into prepared pan.

5 Roll out marzipan on icing-sugared surface to form 20cm x 30cm rectangle; cover dark cake layer with marzipan.

6 Preheat oven to slow.

7 Spread light cake layer evenly over marzipan; bake in slow oven 1 hour. Cover with foil; bake, covered, in slow oven further 1 hour.

8 Brush cake top with extra rum. Cover with foil; cool in pan.

light layer Beat butter, sugar and eggs in small bowl with electric mixer until light and fluffy. Mixture may curdle at this point but will come together later. Stir in flour, rum, fruit and nuts.

SERVES 24

tip Cake will keep for 1 month if stored in an airtight container.

2 cups (340g) seeded dates, chopped coarsely
1 cup (170g) seeded prunes, chopped coarsely
1 cup (150g) dried currants
1/3 cup (80ml) dark rum
40g butter
1/2 cup (100g) firmly packed brown sugar
2 eggs
1/2 cup (50g) pecans, chopped finely
40g dark chocolate, grated finely
1/2 cup (75g) plain flour
1/2 teaspoon bicarbonate of soda
200g marzipan
2 tablespoons icing sugar mixture
1/4 cup (60ml) dark rum, extra

LIGHT LAYER

90g butter, softened
2/3 cup (150g) caster sugar
2 eggs
1 cup (150g) plain flour
1/3 cup (80ml) dark rum
3/4 cup (120g) sultanas
1/2 cup (85g) mixed peel
1/4 cup (55g) finely chopped glacé pineapple
1/2 cup (50g) pecans, chopped finely

Rolling marzipan into rectangle

Cover dark cake layer with marzipan sheet

Spread light cake layer over marzipan

coffee hazelnut torte

PREPARATION TIME 20 MINUTES (plus cooling time)
COOKING TIME 1 HOUR 30 MINUTES

6 egg whites
1¹/₄ cups (275g) caster sugar
¹/₂ cup (75g) roasted hazelnuts,
   chopped coarsely
1 cup (80g) roasted
   flaked almonds
1 tablespoon cocoa powder

COFFEE CREAM

²/₃ cup (160ml) water
1 cup (220g) caster sugar
1 teaspoon gelatine
2 tablespoons milk
1 tablespoon instant
   coffee powder
250g unsalted butter, softened
1 teaspoon vanilla essence

1 Preheat oven to slow. Line three oven trays with baking paper; draw a 22cm-diameter circle on each tray.

2 Beat egg whites in medium bowl with electric mixer until soft peaks form. Gradually add sugar, beating after each addition, until sugar dissolves; fold in hazelnuts.

3 Spread mixture equally on drawn circles; bake in slow oven about 1 hour or until firm. Cool meringues in oven with door ajar.

4 Place one meringue on serving plate; spread with a quarter of the coffee cream. Top with another meringue; spread with a third of the remaining coffee cream. Top with last meringue; coat side of cake with remaining coffee cream. Press almonds over cream all around torte; dust with sifted cocoa.

coffee cream Combine the water, sugar, gelatine, milk and coffee powder in small saucepan; stir over heat, without boiling, until sugar and gelatine dissolve. Cool to room temperature. Beat butter and essence in small bowl with electric mixer until light and fluffy. With motor operating, gradually beat in sugar mixture until fluffy (this will take about 10 minutes).

SERVES 16

tip Trace around a cake pan to get a circle that is the right size.

*hazelnuts, sometimes known as filberts,
can be purchased finely ground and used
in place of flour in some recipes*

sticky date roll with butterscotch sauce

PREPARATION TIME 15 MINUTES • COOKING TIME 30 MINUTES

1 Preheat oven to moderate. Grease 25cm x 30cm swiss roll pan; line base and short sides of pan with baking paper, bringing paper 5cm above edges of pan. Place a piece of baking paper cut the same size as swiss roll pan on board or bench; sprinkle evenly with white sugar.

2 Combine dates, the water and soda in bowl of food processor. Place lid in position; stand 5 minutes. Add butter and brown sugar; process until almost smooth. Add eggs and flour; process until just combined. Pour mixture into prepared pan; bake in moderate oven about 15 minutes.

3 Turn cake onto sugared paper, peel baking paper away; working quickly, use serrated knife to cut away crisp edges from all sides.

4 Using hands and sugared paper as a guide, gently roll cake loosely from a long side; hold for 30 seconds then unroll. Cover cake with tea towel; cool.

5 Beat cream in small bowl with electric mixer until firm peaks form. Fold 1/4 cup of the butterscotch sauce into cream. Spread cake evenly with cream mixture. Roll cake, from same long side, by lifting paper and using it to guide the roll into shape. Serve sticky date roll drizzled with remaining warmed butterscotch sauce.

butterscotch sauce Combine ingredients in small saucepan; stir over heat until sugar dissolves and butter melts.

SERVES 12

tip Rolling and unrolling the cake, then cooling it flat, is not the traditional method for a swiss roll; however, our method helps minimise the likelihood of the cake splitting.

2 tablespoons white sugar
1 cup (160g) seeded dates
3/4 cup (180ml) boiling water
1 teaspoon bicarbonate of soda
50g butter, chopped
2/3 cup (150g) firmly packed brown sugar
2 eggs
3/4 cup (110g) self-raising flour
300ml thickened cream

BUTTERSCOTCH SAUCE

1/2 cup (100g) firmly packed brown sugar
2/3 cup (160ml) thickened cream
100g butter, chopped

Gently roll cake from long side

Roll filled cake using paper to guide into roll

pistachio shortbread mounds

PREPARATION TIME 25 MINUTES • COOKING TIME 25 MINUTES

1/2 cup (75g) roasted
shelled pistachios
250g butter, chopped
1 cup (160g) icing sugar mixture
1 1/2 cups (225g) plain flour
2 tablespoons rice flour
2 tablespoons cornflour
3/4 cup (90g) almond meal
1/3 cup (55g) icing sugar
mixture, extra

1 Preheat oven to slow. Lightly grease two oven trays.

2 Toast nuts in small heavy-based frying pan until lightly browned; remove from pan. Coarsely chop 1/3 cup (50g) of the nuts; leave remaining nuts whole.

3 Beat butter and sugar in small bowl with electric mixer until light and fluffy; transfer mixture to large bowl. Stir in sifted flours, almond meal and chopped nuts.

4 Shape level tablespoons of mixture into mounds; place mounds on prepared trays, allowing 3cm between each mound. Press one reserved nut on each mound; bake in slow oven about 25 minutes or until firm. Stand mounds 5 minutes; transfer to wire rack to cool. Serve mounds dusted with extra sifted icing sugar.

MAKES 40

tip Rice flour, also known as ground rice, is a very fine powder made from pulverised long-grain or glutinous rice. It's used to make noodles and breads, and helps thicken cakes and puddings.

Toast pistachios in a small frying pan

Beat butter and egg mixture until fluffy

Shape tablespoons of mixture into mounds

choc-hazelnut cookie sandwiches

PREPARATION TIME 25 MINUTES (plus refrigeration time)
COOKING TIME 10 MINUTES

Nutella is a commercial spread made of milk chocolate and hazelnuts; it can be used in cooking, as here, or spread on your breakfast toast.

1 Preheat oven to moderate. Lightly grease two oven trays.

2 Beat butter, essence, sugar and egg in small bowl with electric mixer until light and fluffy; stir in hazelnut meal with sifted flour and cocoa. Enclose dough in plastic wrap; refrigerate about 1 hour or until firm.

3 Roll dough between two sheets of baking paper until 3mm thick. Using 4cm-fluted cutter, cut rounds from dough. Place rounds on prepared trays; bake in moderate oven about 8 minutes. Stand biscuits 5 minutes; transfer onto wire rack to cool.

4 Spoon choc-hazelnut cream into piping bag fitted with large fluted tube. Pipe cream onto one biscuit; sandwich with another biscuit. Place on wire rack set over tray; repeat with remaining biscuits and cream. When all sandwiches are on rack, dust with extra sifted cocoa.

choc-hazelnut cream Beat cooled chocolate, butter and Nutella in small bowl with electric mixer until thick and glossy.

MAKES 30

80g butter, chopped
1 teaspoon vanilla essence
1/4 cup (55g) caster sugar
1 egg
1/2 cup (50g) hazelnut meal
3/4 cup (110g) plain flour
1/4 cup (25g) cocoa powder
1 tablespoon cocoa powder, extra

CHOC-HAZELNUT CREAM
100g dark chocolate, melted
50g butter
1/3 cup (110g) Nutella

Completely enclose dough in plastic wrap

Cut 4cm fluted rounds from dough

Pipe cream onto half of the biscuits

cubes of chocolate-coated caramel inject a flavour surprise to these cookies

1 egg
²/₃ cup (150g) firmly packed brown sugar
¹/₄ cup (60ml) vegetable oil
¹/₂ cup (75g) plain flour
¹/₃ cup (50g) self-raising flour
¹/₄ teaspoon bicarbonate of soda
100g dark chocolate, melted
250g Caramello chocolate squares

caramello chocolate cookies

PREPARATION TIME 15 MINUTES • COOKING TIME 20 MINUTES

1 Preheat oven to moderate. Lightly grease two oven trays.

2 Beat egg, sugar and oil in small bowl with electric mixer until mixture changes in colour. Stir in sifted dry ingredients and dark chocolate; stir until mixture becomes firm.

3 Centre one Caramello square on 1 heaped teaspoon chocolate mixture; roll into ball, enclosing Caramello. Place balls on prepared trays, allowing 6cm between each cookie; bake in moderate oven about 10 minutes. Stand cookies 5 minutes; transfer to wire rack to cool.

MAKES 24

tips One heaped teaspoon is equivalent to 3 level teaspoons.
Chocolate squares with strawberry or peppermint centres can be used instead of Caramello squares.
Biscuit dough is suitable to freeze.

pressing biscuits with a fork helps flatten them and gives them a pretty appearance

passionfruit butter yoyo bites

PREPARATION TIME 20 MINUTES • COOKING TIME 15 MINUTES

1 Preheat oven to moderately slow. Line two oven trays with baking paper.

2 Beat butter, essence and sugar in medium bowl with electric mixer until light and fluffy; stir in sifted dry ingredients, in two batches.

3 Roll rounded teaspoons of mixture into balls; place on prepared trays, allowing 3cm between each biscuit. Using fork dusted with a little flour, press tines gently onto each biscuit to flatten slightly; bake in moderately slow oven about 12 minutes or until biscuits are firm. Stand biscuits 5 minutes; transfer to wire rack to cool. Serve biscuits sandwiched with passionfruit butter.

passionfruit butter Beat butter and sugar in small bowl with electric mixer until light and fluffy; stir in passionfruit pulp.

MAKES 37

tip One rounded teaspoon is equivalent to 2 level teaspoons.

250g unsalted butter, chopped
1 teaspoon vanilla essence
1/2 cup (80g) icing sugar mixture
11/2 cups (225g) plain flour
1/2 cup (75g) cornflour

PASSIONFRUIT BUTTER

80g unsalted butter
2/3 cup (150g) icing sugar mixture
1 tablespoon passionfruit pulp

almond nougat

PREPARATION TIME 10 MINUTES (plus standing time) • COOKING TIME 30 MINUTES

It is important to use a candy thermometer in this recipe in order to get the correct consistency when making the nougat. Rice paper is a fine, edible paper that is very useful in the making of biscuits such as macaroons. Contrary to popular belief, it is not actually made from rice but from the pith of a small tree which grows in Asia. Rice paper can be found in specialist food stores and some delicatessens.

2 sheets rice paper
1/2 cup (175g) honey
1 1/3 cups (300g) caster sugar
2 tablespoons water
1 egg white
2 cups (320g) blanched
almonds, toasted

1 Lightly grease deep 15cm-square cake pan. Trim one sheet of rice paper into 15cm square; line base of pan.

2 Combine honey, sugar and the water in small saucepan; stir over heat, without boiling, until sugar dissolves. Using pastry brush dipped in hot water, brush down side of pan to dissolve any sugar crystals; bring to a boil. Boil, uncovered, without stirring, about 10 minutes or until syrup reaches 164°C on candy thermometer; remove pan immediately from heat. Place thermometer in pan of boiling water; remove from heat to allow thermometer to gradually decrease in temperature.

3 Beat egg white in small heatproof bowl with electric mixer until soft peaks form. With motor operating, add hot syrup to egg white in thin, steady stream.

4 Stir almonds into egg white mixture; spoon into prepared pan. Press mixture firmly into pan. Cut remaining sheet of rice paper large enough to cover top of nougat; press lightly onto nougat. Stand about 2 hours or until cool; cut into 2cm squares.

MAKES 49

tips It is important to cool the nougat at room temperature – refrigeration causes it to soften.
Nougat is best kept in an airtight container at room temperature.
For tips on how to use and maintain your candy thermometer, see page 8.

Syrup should reach 164°C on thermometer

Add hot syrup to egg white while beating

Stir almonds into egg white mixture

almonds are the dominant flavour of most Italian biscuits

amaretti

PREPARATION TIME 15 MINUTES (plus standing time)
COOKING TIME 15 MINUTES

1 cup (125g) almond meal
1 cup (220g) caster sugar
2 egg whites
¼ teaspoon almond essence
20 blanched almonds (20g)

1 Lightly grease two oven trays.

2 Beat almond meal, sugar, egg whites and essence in small bowl with electric mixer for 3 minutes; stand 5 minutes.

3 Spoon mixture into piping bag fitted with 1cm plain tube. Pipe directly onto prepared trays in circular motion from centre out, to make biscuits about 4cm in diameter.

4 Top each biscuit with a nut. Cover trays of unbaked biscuits loosely with foil; stand at room temperature overnight.

5 Preheat oven to moderate; bake biscuits in moderate oven about 12 minutes or until browned lightly. Stand amaretti 5 minutes; transfer to wire rack to cool.

MAKES 20

tip Amaretti can be baked the day they're made, however, they will spread a little more. For best results, stand the amaretti overnight.

Peppermint essence is an extract of distilled peppermint leaves

mint slice bites

PREPARATION TIME 20 MINUTES • COOKING TIME 30 MINUTES

1 Preheat oven to moderate. Grease deep 19cm-square cake pan; line base with baking paper.

2 Combine butter and chocolate in medium saucepan; stir over low heat until chocolate melts. Stir in caster sugar and egg then flour. Spread mixture into prepared pan; bake in moderate oven about 20 minutes. Stand cake in pan 15 minutes; turn onto wire rack to cool.

3 Meanwhile, combine icing sugar, extra butter and essence in small heatproof bowl; gradually stir in enough milk to make mixture form a thick paste. Stir mixture over small saucepan of simmering water until icing is of spreadable consistency. Spread icing over cake; allow to set at room temperature.

4 Using serrated knife, trim crisp edges from cake. Cut cake into 3cm squares; drizzle each square with melted extra chocolate.

MAKES 36

125g butter, chopped

200g dark chocolate, chopped coarsely

$^1/_2$ cup (110g) caster sugar

2 eggs, beaten lightly

$1^1/_4$ cups (185g) plain flour

$1^1/_2$ cups (240g) icing sugar mixture

1 teaspoon butter, extra

$^1/_4$ teaspoon peppermint essence

2 tablespoons milk, approximately

50g dark chocolate, melted, extra

cream cheese-filled brandied dates

PREPARATION TIME 30 MINUTES • COOKING TIME 15 MINUTES

1 Make a shallow cut lengthways in each date (do not cut through); remove and discard seeds. Combine dates in medium bowl with brandy; stand 15 minutes.

2 Meanwhile, beat cheese and icing sugar in small bowl with wooden spoon; stir in nuts.

3 Drain brandy from dates into cheese mixture; stir until filling mixture is smooth.

4 Spoon filling mixture into piping bag fitted with small plain tube; pipe mixture into date cavities.

5 Combine caster sugar and the water in small saucepan, stir over heat, without boiling, until sugar dissolves; bring to a boil. Reduce heat; simmer, uncovered, without stirring, until mixture is golden in colour. Remove from heat; stand until bubbles subside.

6 Drizzle half of the dates with toffee and remaining dates with chocolate; allow to set at room temperature.

MAKES 24

tip Toffee is best made just before serving or up to 1 hour beforehand.

24 fresh dates (500g)
1/4 cup (60ml) brandy
125g cream cheese, softened
1 tablespoon icing sugar mixture
1/4 cup (35g) hazelnuts, toasted, chopped finely
1/2 cup (110g) caster sugar
1/4 cup (60ml) water
50g dark chocolate, melted

Remove and discard seeds from dates

Drizzle half of dates with warm toffee

Drizzle chocolate over half of the dates

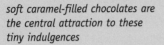

soft caramel-filled chocolates are the central attraction to these tiny indulgences

walnut brownie bites

PREPARATION TIME 15 MINUTES • COOKING TIME 20 MINUTES

1/2 cup (50g) walnuts, toasted,
   chopped finely
80g butter
150g dark chocolate,
   chopped coarsely
3/4 cup (150g) firmly packed
   brown sugar
1 egg, beaten lightly
1/3 cup (50g) plain flour
1/4 cup (60g) sour cream
3 x 50g packets Rolos

1 Preheat oven to moderate. Lightly grease two non-stick 12-hole (11/2-tablespoon) mini muffin pans; divide walnuts among holes.

2 Stir butter and chocolate in small saucepan over low heat until smooth. Stir in sugar; cool to just warm.

3 Stir in egg, then flour and cream; spoon mixture into prepared pan. Press one Rolo into centre of each quantity of mixture; spread mixture so that Rolo is completely enclosed. Bake in moderate oven about 15 minutes. Using a sharp-pointed knife, loosen sides of brownies from pan; stand 10 minutes. Remove brownies gently from pan.

MAKES 24

tip These treats are best served while still warm.

flaked almonds are paper-thin slices ideal for desserts

mini florentines

PREPARATION TIME 10 MINUTES • COOKING TIME 6 MINUTES

1 Preheat oven to moderate. Line two oven trays with baking paper.

2 Combine sultanas, corn flakes, nuts, cherries and milk in medium bowl.

3 Drop heaped teaspoons of mixture onto prepared trays, allowing 5cm between each florentine; bake in moderate oven about 6 minutes or until browned lightly. Cool on trays.

4 Spread half of the bases with white chocolate and remaining half with dark chocolate; run fork through chocolate to make waves. Allow chocolate to set at room temperature.

MAKES 45

tip One heaped teaspoon is equivalent to 3 level teaspoons.

³/₄ cup (120g) sultanas

2 cups (60g) corn flakes

³/₄ cup (60g) flaked
  almonds, toasted

¹/₂ cup (110g) red
  glacé cherries

²/₃ cup (160ml) sweetened
  condensed milk

60g white chocolate, melted

60g dark chocolate, melted

caramel chews

PREPARATION TIME 10 MINUTES • COOKING TIME 15 MINUTES

1 Grease deep 15cm-square cake pan; line base and sides with baking paper.

2 Combine butter, milk, honey and sugar in medium saucepan; stir over heat, without boiling, until sugar dissolves. Increase heat; cook, stirring, about 10 minutes or until glossy and caramel in colour.

3 Pour caramel into prepared pan; cool. Remove caramel from pan. Spread with chocolate; top with nuts. Allow chocolate to set at room temperature; cut into small squares to serve.

MAKES 50

tip You'll know that the caramel is ready to be removed from the heat when the mixture starts to come away from the base and side of the saucepan.

125g butter, chopped
395g can sweetened
   condensed milk
2 tablespoons honey
3/4 cup (150g) firmly packed
   brown sugar
100g dark chocolate, melted
1/4 cup (35g) hazelnuts, toasted,
   chopped coarsely

brown sugar is also good sprinkled over breakfast cereal or fresh fruit

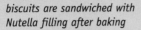

*biscuits are sandwiched with
Nutella filling after baking*

chocolate melting moments

PREPARATION TIME 15 MINUTES • COOKING TIME 10 MINUTES

*Nutella is a commercial spread made of milk chocolate and hazelnuts;
it can be used in cooking, as here, or spread on your breakfast toast.*

125g butter, chopped
2 tablespoons icing sugar mixture
³/₄ cup (110g) plain flour
2 tablespoons cornflour
2 tablespoons cocoa powder
¹/₄ cup (85g) Nutella

1 Preheat oven to moderate. Lightly grease two oven trays.

2 Beat butter and sugar in small bowl with electric mixer until light
and fluffy. Stir in sifted dry ingredients, in two batches.

3 Spoon mixture into piping bag fitted with 5mm fluted tube.
Pipe directly onto prepared trays, allowing 3cm between each biscuit;
bake in moderate oven about 10 minutes or until biscuits are firm.
Stand biscuits 5 minutes; transfer to wire rack to cool. Sandwich
biscuits with Nutella to serve.

MAKES 28

tip Strawberry or raspberry jam can also be used instead of Nutella.

chocolate bits and Melts are handy for baking

triple-choc cookies

PREPARATION TIME 10 MINUTES • COOKING TIME 10 MINUTES

Serve these cookies with hot chocolate for a late-night treat.

1 Preheat oven to moderate. Lightly grease two oven trays.

2 Beat butter, essence, sugar and egg in small bowl with electric mixer until smooth; do not overbeat. Stir in sifted dry ingredients, then raisins and all chocolates.

3 Drop level tablespoons of mixture onto prepared trays, allowing 5cm between each cookie; bake in moderate oven about 10 minutes. Stand cookies 5 minutes; transfer to wire rack to cool.

MAKES 36

tips For a firmer cookie, bake an extra 2 minutes.
Choc Bits are made of cocoa liquor, cocoa butter, sugar and an emulsifier; these hold their shape in baking.
Chocolate Melts are discs of compounded chocolate ideal for melting and moulding.

125g butter, chopped
1/2 teaspoon vanilla essence
11/4 cups (250g) firmly packed brown sugar
1 egg
1 cup (150g) plain flour
1/4 cup (35g) self-raising flour
1 teaspoon bicarbonate of soda
1/3 cup (35g) cocoa powder
1/2 cup (85g) chopped raisins
1/2 cup (95g) milk Choc Bits
1/2 cup (75g) white chocolate Melts, halved
1/2 cup (75g) dark chocolate Melts, halved

lime meringue tartlets

PREPARATION TIME 25 MINUTES • COOKING TIME 15 MINUTES

Pastry shells are made from shortcrust pastry and can be found at some supermarkets. They may be frozen in an airtight container.

1 Combine egg yolks, sugar, rind, juice and butter in small heatproof bowl. Stir constantly over small saucepan of simmering water until mixture thickens slightly and coats the back of a spoon; remove from heat. Cover; refrigerate curd until cold.

2 Preheat oven to hot.

3 Divide curd evenly among pastry shells. Beat egg whites in small bowl with electric mixer until soft peaks form; gradually add extra sugar, 1 tablespoon at a time, beating until sugar dissolves between additions. Gently fold in 1/2 cup (35g) of the coconut.

4 Spoon meringue evenly over curd to enclose filling. Sprinkle tarts with remaining coconut; bake in hot oven about 5 minutes or until meringue is browned lightly. Refrigerate until ready to serve.

MAKES 20

2 eggs, separated
2 tablespoons caster sugar
1 teaspoon finely grated lime rind
1¹/2 tablespoons lime juice
20g butter
20 x 4cm pastry shells
1/2 cup (110g) caster sugar, extra
2/3 cup (50g) shredded coconut

Stir curd constantly until thickened

Beat egg white only until soft peaks form

Spoon meringue onto curd to enclose filling

éclairs, profiteroles and paris-brest

PREPARATION TIME FOR EACH 10 MINUTES
COOKING TIME FOR EACH 30 MINUTES

choux pastry

20g butter
1/4 cup (60ml) water
1/4 cup (35g) plain flour
1 egg

1 Preheat oven to hot. Lightly grease two oven trays.

2 Combine butter with the water in small saucepan; bring to a boil. Add flour; beat with wooden spoon over heat until mixture comes away from base and side of saucepan and forms a smooth ball.

3 Transfer mixture to small bowl; beat in egg with electric mixer until mixture becomes glossy.

4 Spoon mixture into piping bag fitted with 1cm plain tube; proceed with éclair, profiterole or paris-brest recipes.

pastry cream

1 cup (250ml) milk
1/2 vanilla bean, split
3 egg yolks
1/3 cup (75g) caster sugar
2 tablespoons cornflour

1 Bring milk, with vanilla bean added, to a boil in small saucepan. Discard vanilla bean.

2 Meanwhile, beat egg yolks, sugar and cornflour in small bowl with electric mixer until thick. With motor operating, gradually beat in milk mixture. Return custard mixture to saucepan; stir over heat until mixture boils and thickens.

tip To prevent skin forming on the pastry cream, place a piece of plastic wrap over the entire surface until ready to use.

toffee

1 cup (220g) caster sugar
1/2 cup (125ml) water

1 Combine sugar with the water in medium heavy-based frying pan. Stir over heat, without boiling, until sugar dissolves; bring to a boil.

2 Reduce heat; simmer, uncovered, without stirring, until mixture is golden-brown in colour. Remove from heat; stand until bubbles subside and toffee runs evenly from back of spoon.

Choux pastry mixture will come away from side of pan and form a ball

Beat choux pastry mixture until glossy

Pipe 5cm lengths of pastry mixture for éclairs

paris-brest

This sweet, which looks more like a puffy doughnut than a bicycle wheel, was created by a French chef in honour of the famous annual bicycle race run between the two cities of Paris and Brest. In this variation, line trays with baking paper then draw eight 4cm-circles on each tray.

1 Pipe choux pastry mixture around edge of each circle; bake in hot oven 7 minutes. Reduce heat to moderate; bake further 10 minutes or until pastry rings are browned lightly and crisp. Cut each in half horizontally; bake further 5 minutes or until rings are dried out. Cool to room temperature.

2 Spoon pastry cream into piping bag fitted with 1cm plain tube; pipe cream into 16 ring halves; top with remaining halves. Place paris-brest on foil-covered tray. Drizzle with toffee; top with 1/4 cup (20g) flaked almonds.

MAKES 16

profiteroles

Small (just a tad bigger than bite-sized) balls of choux pastry, profiteroles can be sweet or savoury, depending on your choice of filling and topping.

1 Pipe small dollops of choux pastry 5cm apart onto prepared trays; bake in hot oven 7 minutes. Reduce heat to moderate; bake further 10 minutes or until profiteroles are browned lightly and crisp. Cut small opening in side of each profiterole; bake further 5 minutes or until profiteroles are dried out. Cool to room temperature.

2 Spoon pastry cream into piping bag fitted with 1cm plain tube; pipe cream through cuts into profiteroles. Place profiteroles on foil-covered tray; drizzle with toffee.

MAKES 24

mini chocolate éclairs

An éclair is a small, delicate, log-shaped pastry, filled with either pastry cream (crème pâtissière) or fresh whipped cream, and topped with chocolate, toffee, or glacé icing.

1 Pipe 5cm lengths of choux pastry mixture 3cm apart onto prepared trays; bake in hot oven 7 minutes. Reduce heat to moderate; bake further 10 minutes or until éclairs are browned lightly and crisp. Carefully cut eclairs in half, remove any soft centre; bake further 5 minutes or until éclairs are dried out. Cool to room temperature.

2 Spoon pastry cream into piping bag filled with 1cm plain tube; pipe cream onto 16 éclair halves; top with remaining halves. Place éclairs on foil-covered tray; spread with about 60g of melted dark chocolate.

MAKES 16

chocolate panforte

PREPARATION TIME 15 MINUTES • COOKING TIME 55 MINUTES

Rice paper is a fine, edible paper that is very useful in the making of biscuits, such as macaroons. Contrary to popular belief, it is not actually made from rice but from the pith of a small tree which grows in Asia. Rice paper can be found in specialist food stores and some delicatessens.

1 Preheat oven to moderately slow. Grease 20cm sandwich pan; line base with rice paper sheets.

2 Sift flour, cocoa and spices into large bowl; stir in fruit and nuts. Combine honey, sugars and the water in small saucepan; stir over heat, without boiling, until sugar dissolves. Simmer; uncovered, without stirring, 5 minutes. Pour hot syrup then chocolate into nut mixture; stir until well combined. Press mixture firmly into prepared pan. Bake in moderately slow oven about 45 minutes; cool in pan.

3 Remove panforte from pan; wrap in foil. Stand overnight; cut into thin wedges to serve.

MAKES 30

2 sheets rice paper
3/4 cup (110g) plain flour
2 tablespoons cocoa powder
1/2 teaspoon ground cinnamon
1/2 teaspoon ground ginger
1/2 cup (150g) coarsely chopped glacé figs
1/2 cup (85g) dates, halved
1/2 cup (125g) coarsely chopped glacé peaches
1/4 cup (50g) red glacé cherries, halved
1/4 cup (50g) green glacé cherries, halved
1/2 cup (80g) blanched almonds, toasted
1/2 cup (75g) unsalted cashews, toasted
1/2 cup (75g) hazelnuts, toasted
1/2 cup (75g) macadamia nuts, toasted
1/3 cup (115g) honey
1/3 cup (75g) caster sugar
1/3 cup (75g) firmly packed brown sugar
2 tablespoons water
100g dark chocolate, melted

Line pan with both rice paper sheets

Pour hot syrup into the fruit and nut mixture

Press mixture firmly into prepared pan

**360g white chocolate,
chopped coarsely
1/2 cup (140g) smooth
peanut butter
400g dark chocolate,
chopped coarsely**

chocolate and
peanut butter swirl

PREPARATION TIME 15 MINUTES • COOKING TIME 10 MINUTES

1 Grease 20cm x 30cm lamington pan; line base and sides with baking paper, extending 5cm above long edges of pan.

2 Stir white chocolate in small heatproof bowl over small saucepan of simmering water until smooth; cool 5 minutes. Add peanut butter; stir until smooth.

3 Stir dark chocolate in small heatproof bowl over small saucepan of simmering water until smooth; cool slightly.

4 Drop alternate spoonfuls of white chocolate mixture and dark chocolate into prepared pan. Gently shake pan to level mixture; pull a skewer backwards and forwards through mixtures several times for a marbled effect. Stand at room temperature about 2 hours or until set; cut into small pieces.

MAKES ABOUT 72

tip You can melt the chocolate in a microwave oven; cook on MEDIUM (55%) about 1 minute, stirring twice while cooking.

Drop both mixtures by the spoonful into pan

Shake the pan to level mixture

Marble the mixture using a skewer

chocolate cases with mascarpone and berries

PREPARATION TIME 30 MINUTES

We used Grand Marnier in this recipe, but you can use Cointreau or any other orange-flavoured liqueur, if you prefer. You need a small, unused paintbrush for this recipe. Paper cases can be found in confectionery stores and some supermarkets.

1 Lightly spray paper cases with cooking-oil spray. Using small, new, cleaned brush, paint chocolate thickly inside each case. Place paper cases on tray; refrigerate about 5 minutes or until chocolate sets. Peel away and discard paper cases.

2 Meanwhile, combine mascarpone and liqueur in small bowl. Place 1 teaspoon of the mascarpone mixture in each chocolate case; top with berries.

MAKES 16

tip Originally from Lombardy in southern Italy, mascarpone is a buttery-rich, cream-like cheese made from cow milk. Ivory-coloured, soft and delicate, with the texture of softened butter, mascarpone is one of the traditional ingredients in tiramisu and other Italian desserts.

16 x 2.5cm paper cases
cooking-oil spray
100g dark chocolate Melts, melted
1/2 cup (140g) mascarpone cheese
1 tablespoon orange-flavoured liqueur
100g fresh raspberries
100g fresh blueberries

Paint chocolate thickly inside the cases

Peel the cases away carefully

Fill chocolate cases with mixture

chocolate cream fudge

PREPARATION TIME 5 MINUTES (plus standing time)
COOKING TIME 40 MINUTES

It is important to use a candy thermometer in this recipe in order to get the correct consistency when making the fudge. Glucose syrup, also known as liquid glucose, is made from wheat starch. It is mostly used in confectionery and is available at health food stores and supermarkets.

1½ cups (330g) caster sugar

½ cup (100g) firmly packed
   brown sugar

60g dark chocolate,
   chopped coarsely

2 tablespoons glucose syrup

½ cup (125ml) cream

¼ cup (60ml) milk

40g butter

1 Grease deep 15cm-square cake pan.

2 Combine sugars, chocolate, syrup, cream and milk in small saucepan; stir over heat, without boiling, until sugar dissolves. Using pastry brush dipped in hot water, brush down side of pan to dissolve any sugar crystals; bring to a boil. Boil, uncovered, without stirring, about 10 minutes or until syrup reaches 116°C on candy thermometer. Remove pan immediately from heat, leaving candy thermometer in syrup; add butter, do not stir. Cool fudge, about 20 minutes or until syrup drops to 40°C on candy thermometer.

3 Stir fudge with wooden spoon about 10 minutes or until a small amount dropped from the spoon holds its shape. Spread fudge into prepared pan; cover with foil. Stand at room temperature about 3 hours or until fudge sets. Turn fudge out of pan; trim edges. Cut into 2cm squares.

MAKES 49

tip For tips on how to use and maintain your candy thermometer see page 8.

Brush down side of pan with hot water

Syrup must reach 116°C on thermometer

Stir until fudge holds its shape

glossary

almond flat, pointed ended nuts with pitted brown shell enclosing a creamy white kernel which is covered by a brown skin.

BLANCHED brown skins removed.

ESSENCE extract.

FLAKED paper-thin slices.

MEAL also known as ground almonds; nuts are powdered to a flour-like texture.

SLIVERED lengthways-cut, small pieces.

slivered almonds

VIENNA toffee-coated nuts.

baking powder raising agent consisting mainly of two parts cream of tartar to one part bicarbonate of soda.

bicarbonate of soda also known as baking soda.

butter use salted or unsalted ("sweet") butter; 125g is equal to 1 stick of butter.

cherry ripe a cherry and coconut bar coated in dark chocolate.

chocolate

CHOC BITS also known as chocolate chips and chocolate morsels; available in milk, white and dark chocolate. These hold their shape in baking and are ideal as a cake decoration.

DARK eating chocolate; made of cocoa liquor, cocoa butter and sugar.

MELTS discs made of milk, white or dark chocolate compound; good for melting and moulding.

MILK primarily for eating.

WHITE eating chocolate.

cinnamon stick dried inner bark of the shoots of a cinnamon tree.

cocoa powder also known, simply, as cocoa; unsweetened, dried, roasted then ground cocoa beans.

coconut

CREAM the first pressing from grated mature coconut flesh.

DESICCATED unsweetened, concentrated, dried shredded coconut.

MILK the second pressing (less rich) from grated mature coconut flesh.

SHREDDED thin strips of dried coconut flesh.

coffee-flavoured liqueur Tia Maria, Kahlua or any generic brand.

cointreau a clear French liqueur, orange-flavoured brandy, 40% alcohol by volume.

colourings many types are available from cake decorating suppliers, craft shops and some supermarkets; all are concentrated. It's best to use a minute amount of any type of colouring first to determine its strength.

corn flakes crisp flakes of corn.

corn syrup a thick sweet syrup made by processing cornstarch; available in light or dark varieties.

cornflour also known as cornstarch; used as a thickening agent in cooking.

cream

SOUR (minimum fat content 35%) a thick, soured cream that is comercially-cultured.

THICKENED (minimum fat content 35%) a whipping cream containing a thickener.

cream cheese (minimum fat content 33%) commonly known as Philadelphia or Philly; a soft cow milk cheese. Sold at supermarkets in bulk and packaged.

dark rum we prefer to use an underproof rum (not overproof) for a more subtle flavour.

dates from the date palm tree and have a sticky texture; sometimes sold already pitted and chopped.

dried currants tiny, almost black raisins so-named after a grape variety that originated in Corinth, Greece.

ferrero rocher a commercial sweet made from hazelnuts and milk chocolate.

figs (dried) the slightly crunchy, dehydrated form of a black or golden fruit. They can be eaten as is or used as an ingredient in savoury dishes or desserts.

flour

PLAIN an all-purpose flour, made from wheat.

SELF-RAISING an all-purpose flour mixed with baking powder in the proportion of 1 cup flour to 2 teaspoons baking powder.

frangelico a hazelnut-flavoured liqueur.

gelatine (gelatin) we used powdered gelatine as a setting agent. It is also available in sheets called leaf gelatine.

glacé cherries also known as candied cherries; cherries cooked in heavy sugar syrup then dried.

glacé pineapple pineapple that has been cooked in heavy sugar syrup then dried.

golden syrup a by-product of refined sugarcane. The variety sold in a squeezable container is not suitable for the recipes in this book.

grand marnier a brandy-based, orange-flavoured liqueur.

hazelnuts also known as filberts; plump, grape-size, rich, sweet nut having a brown inedible skin that is removed by rubbing heated nuts together vigorously in a tea towel.

MEAL also known as ground hazelnuts; the nut is roasted then powdered to a flour-like texture for use in baking.

honey the variety sold in a squeezable container is not suitable for the recipes in this book.

ice-cream we used an ice-cream with 5g of fat per 100ml.

jam also known as preserve or conserve.

kahlua a brandy-based, coffee-flavoured liqueur.

dark and white eating chocolate

choc melts

choc bits

lamington pan a 20cm x 30cm, straight-sided rectangular slab cake pan, 3cm deep.

limoncello an Italian lemon-flavoured liqueur; originally made from the juice and peel of lemons grown along the Amalfi coast.

macadamias native to Australia, a rich and buttery nut; store in the refrigerator because of its high oil content.

maple syrup a thin syrup distilled from the sap of the maple tree.

maple-flavoured syrup made from sugar cane rather than maple-tree sap; used in cooking or as a topping but cannot be considered an exact substitute for pure maple syrup.

marsala a sweet fortified wine originally from Sicily.

marshmallows pink and white; made from sugar, glucose, gelatine and cornflour.

mascarpone a fresh, unripened, thick, triple-cream cheese with a delicately sweet, slightly acidic flavour.

milk we used full-cream homogenised milk unless otherwise specified.

SWEETENED CONDENSED a canned milk product consisting of milk with more than half the water content removed and sugar added to the milk that remains.

mixed peel also known as candied citrus peel.

mixed spice a blend of ground spices usually consisting of cinnamon, allspice and nutmeg.

demerara sugar

caster sugar

brown sugar

icing sugar mixture

nutella a chocolate-hazelnut spread.

peanut butter peanuts ground to a paste; available in crunchy and smooth varieties.

pecans native to the United States and now grown locally; golden-brown, buttery and rich.

pistachio a pale green, delicately flavoured nut inside a hard off-white shell. To peel, soak shelled nuts in boiling water for about 5 minutes; drain then pat dry with absorbent paper. Rub skins with cloth to peel.

prunes commercially- or sun-dried plums.

raisins dried, sweet grapes.

raisin toast a fruit loaf containing raisins, sultanas and currants with a little spice.

rice paper contrary to popular belief, rice paper isn't made from rice but from the pith of a small tree which grows in Asia. The fine, glossy paper is edible and is very useful in the making of biscuits, such as macaroons. This variety, generally imported from Holland, looks like a grainy sheet of white paper. It is used in confectionery making and baking, and can not be eaten uncooked.

rosewater extract made from crushed rose petals, called gulab in India; used for its aromatic quality in many desserts.

sugar

BROWN a soft, fine granulated sugar containing molasses to give its characteristic colour.

CASTER also known as superfine or finely granulated table sugar.

DEMERARA small-grained, golden-coloured crystal sugar.

ICING SUGAR MIXTURE also known as confectioners' sugar or powdered sugar; crushed granulated sugar with added cornflour (about 3%).

PURE ICING also known as confectioners' sugar but without the addition of cornflour.

RAW natural brown granulated sugar

WHITE we used coarse, granulated table sugar, unless otherwise specified.

sultanas also known as golden raisins; dried seedless white grapes.

tequila a colourless alcoholic liquor of Mexican origin made from the fermented sap of the agave, a succulent desert plant.

tia maria a coffee-flavoured liqueur.

vanilla
BEAN dried long, thin pod from a tropical golden orchid grown in Central and South America and Tahiti; the minuscule black seeds inside the bean are used to impart a luscious vanilla flavour in baking and desserts.

ESSENCE distilled from the seeds of the vanilla pod; imitation vanilla extract is not a satisfactory substitute.

vegetable oil any of a number of oils sourced from plants rather than animal fats

walnuts are rich, crisp-textured nuts with crinkled surfaces and an astringent flavour

pecans

index

facts and figures

Wherever you live, you'll be able to use our recipes with the help of these easy-to-follow conversions. While these conversions are approximate only, the difference between an exact and the approximate conversion of various liquid and dry measures is but minimal and will not affect your cooking results.

helpful measures

The difference between one country's measuring cups and another's is, at most, within a 2 or 3 teaspoon variance. (For the record, one Australian metric measuring cup holds approximately 250ml.) The most accurate way of measuring dry ingredients is to weigh them. When measuring liquids, use a clear glass or plastic jug with the metric markings. (One Australian metric tablespoon holds 20ml; one Australian metric teaspoon holds 5ml.)

If you would like to purchase *The Australian Women's Weekly* Test Kitchen's metric measuring cups and spoons (as approved by Standards Australia), turn to page 120 for details and order coupon. You will receive:

- a graduated set of four cups for measuring dry ingredients, with sizes marked on the cups.
- a graduated set of four spoons for measuring dry and liquid ingredients, with amounts marked on the spoons.

Note: North America, NZ and the UK use 15ml tablespoons. All cup and spoon measurements are level.

We use large eggs having an average weight of 60g.

how to measure

When using graduated metric measuring cups, shake dry ingredients loosely into the appropriate cup.
Do not tap the cup on a bench or tightly pack the ingredients unless directed to do so. Level top of measuring cups and measuring spoons with a knife. When measuring liquids, place a clear glass or plastic jug with metric markings on a flat surface to check accuracy at eye level.

dry measures

metric	imperial
15g	1/2oz
30g	1oz
60g	2oz
90g	3oz
125g	4oz (1/4lb)
155g	5oz
185g	6oz
220g	7oz
250g	8oz (1/2lb)
280g	9oz
315g	10oz
345g	11oz
375g	12oz (3/4lb)
410g	13oz
440g	14oz
470g	15oz
500g	16oz (1lb)
750g	24oz (1 1/2lb)
1kg	32oz (2lb)

liquid measures

metric	imperial
30ml	1 fluid oz
60ml	2 fluid oz
100ml	3 fluid oz
125ml	4 fluid oz
150ml	5 fluid oz (1/4 pint/1 gill)
190ml	6 fluid oz
250ml	8 fluid oz
300ml	10 fluid oz (1/2 pint)
500ml	16 fluid oz
600ml	20 fluid oz (1 pint)
1000ml (1 litre)	1 3/4 pints

helpful measures

metric	imperial
3mm	1/8in
6mm	1/4in
1cm	1/2in
2cm	3/4in
2.5cm	1in
5cm	2in
6cm	2 1/2in
8cm	3in
10cm	4in
13cm	5in
15cm	6in
18cm	7in
20cm	8in
23cm	9in
25cm	10in
28cm	11in
30cm	12in (1ft)

Looking after **your interest...**

Keep your ACP cookbooks clean, tidy and within easy reach with slipcovers designed to hold up to 12 books. Plus you can follow our recipes perfectly with a set of accurate measuring cups and spoons, as used by *The Australian Women's Weekly* Test Kitchen.

To order

Mail or fax Photocopy and complete the coupon below and post to ACP Books Reader Offer, ACP Publishing, GPO Box 4967, Sydney NSW 2001, or fax to (02) 9267 4967.

Phone Have your credit card details ready, then phone 136 116 (Mon-Fri, 8.00am-6.00pm; Sat, 8.00am-6.00pm).

Price

Book Holder

Australia: $13.10 (incl. GST).
Elsewhere: $A21.95.

Metric Measuring Set

Australia: $6.50 (incl. GST).
New Zealand: $A8.00.
Elsewhere: $A9.95.

Prices include postage and handling. This offer is available in all countries.

Payment

Australian residents

We accept the credit cards listed on the coupon, money orders and cheques.

Overseas residents

We accept the credit cards listed on the coupon, drafts in $A drawn on an Australian bank, and also British, New Zealand and U.S. cheques in the currency of the country of issue. Credit card charges are at the exchange rate current at the time of payment.

Photocopy and complete coupon below

- -

☐ **Book Holder**

☐ **Metric Measuring Set**
   Please indicate number(s) required.

Mr/Mrs/Ms _____

Address _____

_____

Postcode _____ Country _____

Ph: Business hours (   ) _____

I enclose my cheque/money order for $ _____ payable to ACP Publishing.

OR: please charge my

☐ Bankcard   ☐ Visa   ☐ Mastercard
☐ Diners Club   ☐ American Express

Card number | | | | | | | | | | | | | | | | | | |

Card number

Expiry date ____ /____

Cardholder's signature _____

Please allow up to 30 days delivery within Australia.
Allow up to 6 weeks for overseas deliveries.
Both offers expire 31/12/02. HLWSI02

Designer *Alison Windmill*
Editor *Deborah Quick*

Test Kitchen Staff
Food director *Pamela Clark*
Food editor *Karen Hammial*
Assistant food editor *Amira Ibram*
Test kitchen manager *Elizabeth Hooper*
Senior home economist *Kimberley Coverdale*
Home economists *Kellie Ann,*
Kelly Cruickshanks, Sarah Hobbs,
Cathie Lonnie, Naomi Scesny,
Alison Webb, Danielle West
Editorial coordinator *Amanda Josling*
Home economists for photography
Kelly Cruickshanks, Kimberley Coverdale
Step photography *Rob Shaw*

ACP Books Staff
Editorial director *Susan Tomnay*
Creative director *Hieu Nguyen*
Senior editors *Julie Collard, Liz Neate*
Senior writer and editor *Lynda Wilton*
Editor *Deborah Quick*
Designers *Mary Keep, Caryl Wiggins,*
Alison Windmill
Studio manager *Caryl Wiggins*
Editorial coordinator *Holly van Oyen*
Editorial assistant *Lana Meldrum*
Publishing manager (sales)
Jennifer McDonald
Publishing manager (rights & new projects)
Jane Hazell
Assistant brand manager *Donna Gianniotis*
Pre-press *Harry Palmer*
Production manager *Carol Currie*
Business manager *Sally Lees*

Chief executive officer *John Alexander*
Group publisher Jill Baker
Publisher *Sue Wannan*

Produced by ACP Books, Sydney.
Printed by Dai Nippon Printing in Korea.
Published by ACP Publishing Pty Limited,
54 Park St, Sydney; GPO Box 4088,
Sydney, NSW 1028.
Ph: (02) 9282 8618 Fax: (02) 9267 9438.
acpbooks@acp.com.au
www.acpbooks.com.au
To order books, phone 136 116.
Send recipe enquiries to
recipeenquiries@acp.com.au
AUSTRALIA: Distributed by Network Services,
GPO Box 4088, Sydney, NSW 1028.
Ph: (02) 9282 8777 Fax: (02) 9264 3278.
UNITED KINGDOM: Distributed by Australian
Consolidated Press (UK), Moulton Park
Business Centre, Red House Rd, Moulton Park,
Northampton, NN3 6AQ
Ph: (01604) 497 531 Fax: (01604) 497 533
acpukltd@aol.com
CANADA: Distributed by Whitecap Books Ltd,
351 Lynn Ave, North Vancouver, BC,
V7J 2C4, Ph: (604) 980 9852.
NEW ZEALAND: Distributed by Netlink
Distribution Company, Level 4, 23 Hargreaves S
College Hill, Auckland 1, Ph: (9) 302 7616.
SOUTH AFRICA: Distributed by PSD Promotions
(Pty) Ltd, PO Box 1175, Isando 1600, SA,
Ph: (011) 392 6065.

Wicked
Includes index.
ISBN 1 86396 280 8
1. Desserts. 2. Biscuits. 3. Cake.
I Title: Australian Women's Weekly.
(Series: Australian Women's Weekly).
641.86

© ACP Publishing Pty Limited 2002
ABN 18 053 273 546
This publication is copyright. No part of it may be reproduced or transmitted in any form withou the written permission of the publishers.
First published 2002.
The publishers would like to thank *Peppergreen* in Berrima for help in preparing this book.

CONTENTS

THE MEDIEVAL AGE

THE MIDDLE AGES IN Europe lasted around a thousand years – from roughly AD 500, as Roman power collapsed in western Europe, to 1500, when new forces driven by the Renaissance and Reformation were reshaping European society. Three key elements combined to create medieval society: the importance of kingship, the role of the Christian Church, and the development of a land-based social structure conveniently known as 'feudalism'. These powerful forces shaped a way of life that was in some respects very different from our own, yet with many familiar features.

For England, and ultimately for the whole of Britain, the year 1066 marked a turning point. The Norman Conquest overthrew 500 years of Saxon dominance in England, creating a new social order. Beginning with the story of the Conquest, this book traces the history of medieval England to 1485 and the end of the Wars of the Roses.

An era of English history that began and ended with invasion and a change of king was seldom anything but tumultuous. In a world without newspapers, where news and rumour were spread by gossip and proclamation, there were many dramatic and significant 'stories' such as the sign-ing of Magna Carta, the assassination of Thomas Becket and the mysterious disappearance of the Princes in the Tower. The evocative words of witnesses and commentators, illuminating the dry facts of ancient manuscripts, bring such stories to life, and also highlight the expe-riences of ordinary men and women.

Battles for a crown begin and end the story that opens at Hastings and closes at Bosworth. In both of these conflicts, a reigning king lost his life and throne to a rival. After Bosworth, and as the Middle Ages drew to a close, the new Tudor dynasty arose triumphant to rule England. Another colourful chapter in the long history of these islands had begun to unfold.

MYTH AND REALITY
Myth and reality were never far apart in the Middle Ages. This medieval artist pictured a tour-nament at Caerleon, Wales, in the presence of the legendary King Arthur. People are wearing the armour and court dress of a later age of chivalry.

MEDIEVAL MASTERWORKS
A breathtaking achievement: the soaring nave of Canterbury Cathedral leads the eye heaven-wards to the intricate vaulting of the ceiling. Dating from c. 1400, Canterbury's nave is the work of Henry Yevele, master mason to Edward III.

In 1068, the Normans built a castle on a mound overlooking the River Avon at Warwick. Warwick Castle remains one of the most imposing medieval castles in Britain.

All people in the hierarchy of medieval society knew their rights and duties, from lowly peasant tilling the fields to king enthroned in majesty. Through war, rebellion, famine and pestilence, ordinary people worked to the age-old seasonal and customary rhythms. Life was hard, usually short and sometimes brutal, but sustained by the Christian Church's vision of a better hereafter for the godly.

Topping the pyramid of medieval society was the king. He ruled with God-given authority – his word was law. This ancient creed was reinforced after the Norman Conquest of 1066. William the Conqueror's first requirement was 'that one God be revered throughout his whole realm'; his second was 'that every freeman shall affirm by oath and compact that he will be loyal to King William ... and defend him against all his enemies.'

The Anglo-Saxon Chronicle summed up the Conqueror as 'a very wise man, and very powerful, and more worshipped and stronger than any predecessor had been ... gentle to the good men who loved God, and stern beyond all measure to those who resisted his will.' This was very much the model for medieval kingship.

MONARCHS OF MEDIEVAL BRITAIN: FROM NORMANS TO TUDORS

England		Scotland	
Norman		Malcolm III Canmore	1058 – 93
William I	1066 – 87	Donald Ban	1093 – 94
William II	1087 – 1100	Duncan II	1094
Henry I	1100 – 35	Donald Ban and Edmund	1094 – 97
Stephen	1135 – 54	Edgar	1097 – 1107
Plantagenet		Alexander I	1107 – 24
Henry II	1154 – 89	David I	1124 – 53
Richard I	1189 – 99	Malcolm IV	1153 – 65
John	1199 – 1216	William the Lion	1165 – 1214
Henry III	1216 – 72	Alexander II	1214 – 49
Edward I	1272 – 1307	Alexander III	1249 – 86
Edward II	1307 – 27	Margaret	1286 – 90
Edward III	1327 – 77	John Balliol	1292 – 96
Richard II	1377 – 99	Robert I the Bruce	1306 – 29
Lancaster		David II	1329 – 71
Henry IV	1399 – 1413	Robert II the Steward	1371 – 90
Henry V	1413 – 22	Robert III	1390 – 1406
Henry VI	1422 – 61	James I	1406 – 37
York		James II	1437 – 60
Edward IV	1461 – 83	James III	1460 – 88
Richard III	1483 – 85	James IV	1488 – 1513
Tudor			
Henry VII	1485 – 1509		

SOVEREIGN OVER ALL

A penny coin stamped with the head of William the Conqueror.

Princes of Wales

of Gwynedd (G), Powys (P) and Deheubarth (D)

Rhys Ap Tewdwr (D)	1039 – 63
Gruffydd ap Llywelyn (D and G)	d. 1093
Gruffydd ap Cynan (G)	d. 1137
Madog ap Maredudd (P)	d. 1160
Owain Gwynedd (G)	1137 – 70
Rhys ap Gruffydd (D)	1155 – 97
Dafydd (G)	d. 1194
Llywelyn ap Iorwerth 'the Great'	1196 – 1240
Dafydd ap Llywelyn (II)	1240 – 46
Llywelyn ap Gruffydd 'the Last'	1255 – 82
Dafydd ap Gruffydd	1282 – 83

FROM NORMANS TO PLANTAGENETS

Conqueror commemorated

A statue raised to William the Conqueror at Falaise in his native Normandy. William considered England rightfully his, promised both by Edward and (he claimed) by Harold during a visit to Normandy in either 1064 or 1065.

THE YEAR 1066, most quoted of all dates in English history, saw a decisive step in the evolution of the nation. This was largely the achievement of one man, William the Conqueror. It was his will that drove the Normans across the Channel, to overthrow the Saxon monarchy and set up a new ruling dynasty. The Norman kings and the Plantagenets who succeeded them introduced a French connection, in language, law and landholding, that was to shape Britain's history for the next 400 years.

Between 500 and 1066 a number of kingdoms had emerged in Britain. Saxons settling in the south, along with Angles and other 5th-century Germanic migrants, produced seven 'English' kingdoms: Essex, Wessex, Sussex, Kent, Northumbria, Mercia and East Anglia. In the 9th century, Wessex kings beginning with Alfred repulsed Viking invasion, and their successors achieved supremacy over a united England. But Norse persistence paid off, leading to later Danish rule over England by King Cnut (1016–35) and his sons. Scotland and Wales developed their own kingdoms and principalities, along similar lines.

In 1042, Edward the Confessor restored the old Wessex line of Alfred the Great, but displayed little of his ancestor's tough warrior spirit. Pious, half-Norman Edward had lived mainly

FROM WILLIAM TO STEPHEN

Norman kings show the buildings they left behind in this illustration to a history book by the monk Matthew Paris (d. 1259): William I holds Battle Abbey (top left); William II, Westminster Hall (top right); Henry I, Reading Abbey (bottom left); Stephen, Faversham Abbey (bottom right).

in France. Dominated by ruthless Earl Godwin of Wessex, his main interest lay in rebuilding Westminster Abbey. Edward's Norman allies urged him to make William of Normandy his heir, but when Edward died in January 1066, Godwin's son Harold was picked to succeed him. Across the Channel, an angry Duke William prepared for war to back his contesting claim to the English Crown.

The omens were uncertain, even though *The Anglo-Saxon Chronicle* recorded 'such a token in the heavens as no man ever before saw. Some men said it was cometa, the star which some men call the haired star.' Halley's Comet had arrived as William's herald.

THE BATTLE OF HASTINGS

HAROLD II WAS CROWNED on 6 January 1066. The English saw him as a proven leader, despite his lack of royal ancestry. The Normans regarded Harold as a usurper and oath-breaker. Across the Channel, William of Normandy gathered an invasion fleet but was kept in port by contrary winds. Meanwhile, Harold faced a new threat from his brother Tostig, a malcontent turned freebooter who threw in his lot with Norway's Harald Hardrada to launch yet another Viking attack across the North Sea.

⁓

Harold marched north to meet them. At Stamford Bridge, on Yorkshire's River Derwent, he routed the Scandinavians in a day-long slaughter on 25 September. On 28 September, the Normans landed on the south coast at Pevensey. Flushed with victory, confident, and set on saving his Wessex lands from pillaging invaders, Harold did not wait for reinforcements but moved at once to meet the enemy.

The Battle of Hastings, on 14 October, was fought on Senlac Hill from around 9 a.m. until 4 p.m. Estimates of army numbers vary between 3,000 and 7,000 apiece, with the Normans slightly stronger. Though confident, Harold's warriors lacked archers and cavalry – and must have been weary. Choosing ground on a ridge-top, they formed a human wall, shield to shield. The English might ride horses to the battlefield, but they dismounted to fight, giving themselves room to swing their favourite weapon, a long-handled axe.

⁓

The fighting that followed the first Norman charge was stamina-sapping and bloody. The Anglo-Norman chronicler Wace described how one Norman knight attacked an English soldier, cutting off his right hand. Wace goes on to describe how, as a second Norman sprang forward, the wounded Englishman 'with his long-handled axe struck him over the back, breaking all his bones.'

NORMAN CHARGE

Norman knights charged with lances steadied firmly under their right arms and long shields over the left. At Hastings, Norman armoured cavalry finally broke the disciplined resistance of the English, who fought on foot.

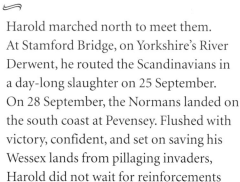

'He charged the Englishman, striking him over the helmet so that it fell down over his eyes; and as he stretched out his hand to raise it, the Norman cut off his right hand.'

Wace (c. 1100–74), describing a
Norman knight's attack

BAYEUX TAPESTRY BATTLE SCENE

This section of the Bayeux Tapestry shows English axemen tackling Norman cavalry. The tapestry, a wool-embroidered panel 75 metres (82 yards) long, was probably made in Canterbury to the order of Bishop Odo, William's half-brother.

For hours the English stood firm, deflecting Norman mounted attacks until, disastrously, men broke ranks to chase fleeing Normans and were cut to pieces. The shield-wall was breached. Harold fell as daylight failed, with his brothers Gurth and Leofwine. The king's bodyguard, brandishing battleaxes, fought to the death.

So ended 500 years of Saxon rule in England. On Christmas Day 1066, the Conqueror was crowned in Edward the Confessor's new abbey at Westminster.

THE NORMAN INVASION

This map of the Norman invasion shows William's route across the Channel to Pevensey. After victory at Hastings, William moved eastwards to Dover and then north to London, where he was crowned King of England.

BLOODY WORK AT HASTINGS

'The sound of the trumpets in both armies was the terrible signal for beginning the battle. **The Normans made the first attack** ... their infantry rushing forward to provoke the English, and **spreading wounds and death** through their ranks **by showers of arrows** ... The English, on their side, made a stout resistance.'

Norman monk Ordericus Vitalis (1075–1142), in his *Historia Ecclesiastica*

NORMAN RULE

NORMAN OCCUPATION FORCES operated from castles commanding the English landscape. 'There were many castles throughout England, each defending their neighbourhood but, more properly, laying it waste,' wrote William of Malmesbury – recording that Norman garrisons drove off sheep and cattle and plundered houses.

~

William crushed all resistance: in 1067 at Exeter and in 1069 in the north. Hereward the Wake's rebels on the Isle of Ely were ruthlessly hunted down although Edric the Wild, leading resistance on the Welsh borders, was pardoned. William moved on Scotland to gain the submission of its king, Malcolm Canmore, in 1072.

We have no realistic likeness of William the Conqueror, but he was evidently a man of impressive bulk as well as commanding manner. King Philip of France said he looked like a pregnant woman. A monk of Caen described him as 'great in body and strong, tall in stature but not ungainly'. The Conqueror was said to be temperate in eating and drinking, and to abhor drunkenness.

~

Not so his son Robert, nicknamed 'Curthose' (short leggings), who according to the chronicler Ordericus Vitalis wasted his means and was addicted to the society of 'harlots and buffoons'. It was even said that the 'idle scamps and loose

DIGGING IN

The Bayeux Tapestry shows Normans building a castle at Hastings after their victory in 1066. The earth motte, or mound, is topped with a wooden palisade. Around the motte was an enclosure, the bailey, normally surrounded by a ditch.

women' with whom Robert kept company frequently made off with his breeches and hose and other articles of dress.

In 1087, the Conqueror died on campaign in defence of Normandy, after his horse stumbled and threw him against the high saddle. William left the duchy of Normandy to his eldest son Robert. England passed to his second son, William, called 'Rufus' (red) because of his fair hair and florid complexion. The third son, Henry, inherited a fortune in silver.

Robert, however, was lazy and dissolute. William Rufus, capable and determined like his father, soon invaded Normandy, which Robert handed over in return for ready money before joining the First Crusade (1096), in which he fought bravely. In Britain, Rufus pushed Norman rule into South Wales and northern England. A skirmish with the Scots in 1093 dispatched King Malcolm, whose three sons were nominated in turn by Rufus to reign in Scotland as his vassals.

The Norman Conquest was complete. Its enduring legacies included those of language, law and architecture. Above all, Norman victory at Hastings wrenched England away from the Scandinavian world, into the mainstream of Europe.

'He was often penniless, and so much in want of clothes that he lay in bed until 12 o'clock and could not go to church to hear mass because he had nothing to wear.'

Ordericus Vitalis, writing about Robert Curthose

CONQUEROR'S CHURCH

Battle Abbey on Senlac Hill was founded by William after his victory at the Battle of Hastings. The high altar is said to mark the spot where Harold fell in 1066.

CONTRITE CONQUEROR

In his deathbed confession, as recorded by Ordericus Vitalis, c. 1130, William expressed remorse for his harrying of the English who were now his subjects: **'I have persecuted the natives of England beyond all reason.** Whether gentle or simple **I have cruelly oppressed them … innumerable multitudes perished through me by famine or the sword … I fell on the English of the northern shires like a ravening lion … and so became the barbarous murderer of many thousands,** both young and old, of that fine race of people. Having gained the throne of that kingdom by so many crimes I dare not leave it to anyone but God.'

FEUDAL ENGLAND

ACROSS ENGLAND, Norman kings built mighty castles and soaring cathedrals. They altered laws and drew internal borders that still exist. Half the words in the language we speak today derive from Norman French. After 1066, Normans took the top jobs formerly held by Englishmen. The occupiers (probably no more than 25,000 during William I's reign) lorded it over some two million English, drawing their power from military dominance and landholding.

About 200 castles were built in 35 years following the Norman Conquest, using local people as forced labour. The castle was a residence as well as a fortress, owned or lived in by the king, a member of his family, a trusted friend or a lord.

William the Conqueror was shrewd in parcelling out land units, called fiefs, to his supporters. Half of all farmland went to Norman nobles and a quarter to the Church. To reinforce the legality of his takeover, William confirmed the laws of Edward the Confessor,

'Likewise the maker of bad beer was either set in the ducking stool or paid 4 shillings to the reeves.'

The Domesday Book

GREAT WHITE TOWER

The Tower of London's massive keep, the White Tower, was begun during William I's reign and completed after his death. It was painted white in 1240.

14

retained Saxon forms of government, and even tried to learn English. English laws were upheld when it suited the new Norman rulers. The 1086 Domesday survey reported that in Chester a man or woman giving false measure in the city paid a fine of 4 shillings. Normal local customs were maintained to ensure that life went on more or less as before. To repair the city walls, the local reeve was empowered to call up one man from each hide to help with the labouring work. A reeve was a local official, while a hide was an area of land for ploughing that varied in extent but was typically around 120 acres.

The Normans were, however, adaptable and they quickly developed a Normanized administration. The government was run by officials with Norman titles such as steward, butler, chamberlain, constable, marshal and chancellor.

Landholding was the basis of Norman feudalism. In the social pyramid, with the king at the top, each tier of society knew its rights and obligations. The king's land was let to barons; barons let lands to knights and freemen; they let lands to peasants, who worked the lord's land and their own. In return for service, the servant expected protection. The new age was one of big landholders: by the time William ordered the Domesday survey of his kingdom, some 200 Normans had replaced over 4,000 Saxon landlords.

DOMESDAY LAMENTS

The Norman Conquest had an unwelcome impact on many people's lives, overturning 500 years of Anglo-Saxon tradition. The Domesday Book highlights the changes, and many English men and women bewailed the loss of land, rights and privileges it detailed. 'Before 1066 he held it himself; now he holds it from William of Ansculf **harshly and wretchedly** [he is now a tenant, not a freeholder].' And from Nottingham ...'They were accustomed to fish in the River Trent, and **now they make complaint because they are forbidden to fish.'**

MAKING MERRY

English nobles enjoyed wine and music. Normans deprived the English lords of their land as they took over to form a new ruling class. Lament for lost liberties remained a persistent theme among the English. But life went on.

THE DOMESDAY BOOK

WILLIAM I VISITED ENGLAND just four times between 1072 and 1087. His last trip (1085–86) was noteworthy for the most astonishing feat of Norman bureaucracy, the survey or inventory we know as the Domesday Book – a unique record of who held which bits of land, and how much it was worth.

Nothing like it, in scale or detail, had been attempted before. Exactly what William wanted is still debated, but a survey of his new realm was obviously useful for tax-raising, and to sort out land-tenure. The king's seven teams of commissioners used existing English tax records to guide them when interviewing landholders. They checked data against evidence given by witnesses from each village in court. Comparisons were drawn between pre-Conquest landholdings in 1066 and those of 1086 – detailing statistics such as ploughed land, mills and fishponds.

PIGS MUST EAT
For the mass of England's peasantry, the Norman Conquest brought little real change. Pigs still had to be driven into the forest to eat acorns knocked down from trees with sticks.

THE BOOK OF JUDGEMENT
The Domesday Book was so nicknamed because, like the Day of Judgement (Doom), none could argue against its findings. The Domesday manuscripts are today kept at The National Archives (Public Record Office), Kew.

'So very narrowly did he have it [the kingdom] investigated, that there was no single hide nor a yard of land, nor indeed ... one ox nor one cow nor one pig was there left out and not put down in his record.'

The Anglo-Saxon Chronicle

DOMESDAY RESIDENCE

Reconstruction of a Saxon house at Bury St Edmunds in Suffolk. When the Domesday Book was compiled, most people in England were living in houses built like this.

In its two volumes, the Domesday Book covers all England except for Durham, Northumberland, Cumberland, Westmorland and northern Lancashire. Great Domesday features all of England south of the Tees-Ribble line, apart from the eastern counties of Essex, Suffolk and Norfolk which appear in Little Domesday. Several related documents also survive. One, the Exon Domesday kept at Exeter, is a draft survey of Somerset, Dorset, Wiltshire, Devon and Cornwall.

Domesday names some 13,000 settlements. For most English villages and towns (though not London or Winchester, whose records have vanished), Domesday is their entry into history.

SECRETS OF COUNTRY FOLK

'In Wallington [Surrey], Fulco holds of Gilbert 3 hides and 40 acres of land. There is land for 5 ploughs ... There is pasture for beasts and wood for hedges ... Altogether it is worth 50s [shillings]. When he received it, 30s. At the time of King Edward, 100s.'

'William de Braose holds Wasingtetune [Washington, West Sussex]. Earl Gyrth held it before 1066 ... 120 villagers and 25 smallholders with 34 ploughs ... 5 salt-houses [presumably beside the nearby River Adur]; 60 pigs; 6 slaves ...'

'Pontefract, then Tateshall [Yorkshire]: Ilbert has there 4 ploughs and 60 petty burgesses, 16 cottagers, 16 villagers and 8 smallholders who have 18 ploughs. A church is there and a priest. 1 fishery. 3 mills ...'

The Domesday Book

FAMILY FEUDS

William the Conqueror, depicted here on a 14th-century manuscript, loved deer-hunting, but it was while they were hunting in the New Forest that two of his sons met their deaths.

THE RUFUS STONE
This marks the spot in the New Forest where William II fell.

'*[Henry I] was extremely fond of the wonders of distant countries, begging with great delight ... from foreign kings, lions, leopards, lynxes or camels – animals which England does not produce.*'

William of Malmesbury

HUNTING KEPT THE NORMANS fit for warfare. They practised it with skill, energy and passion, setting aside vast tracts of land protected by harsh laws. But hunting was risky, and in August 1100 William Rufus was killed in the New Forest, shot in the back. Accident or murder? No one was saying. The person blamed, a man named Walter Tirel, fled abroad. The king's brother Henry, also out hunting, raced to Winchester to grab the treasury – and the Crown. Peasants carted the abandoned Rufus to Winchester where, refused full Church rites (on grounds of moral laxity), he was buried under the cathedral tower.

William II had never married, so three days after his death, his brother Henry was crowned king. There is no proof that Henry had anything to do with Rufus's death, but he undoubtedly profited by it.

Henry I, a shrewd ruler and diplomat, handed over a huge dowry of silver to marry his 11-year-old daughter Matilda to the German (Holy Roman) Emperor in 1114. But it was his son, William, who carried the hopes of the Norman dynasty.

Those hopes died on a cold November night in 1120 when the prince drowned, crossing the Channel in a ship on which almost all the passengers and crew were drunk. Out of 200 people aboard, there was just one survivor.

Henry I holds the record among English kings for illegitimate children (20, at least), whom he cleverly married off to favourable allies. His sorrow at the death of his son was heartfelt, and seemed only to increase his determination to have an heir of his choosing.

A second marriage produced no more children and so Henry's ambitions switched to Matilda. On her return to England after her husband's death in 1125, Henry made his barons swear allegiance to her as his heir, together with 'her lawful husband, should she have one'. The husband materialized in 1128, when 26-year-old Empress Matilda married 15-year-old Geoffrey, Count of Anjou. They were soon separated, but were reunited to produce two sons: Henry, in 1133, and Geoffrey a year later.

Matilda and her husband Geoffrey quarrelled not only with one another, but also with Henry, demanding land, money and castles in characteristic Norman style. The English nobles, reluctant to support a woman, were forced more than once to renew their allegiance to Matilda. They were wary of a king who, they knew, dealt harshly with disloyalty: he had once pushed a man from the top of Rouen Castle for betraying his brother.

When Henry died at a hunting lodge in France in 1135, traditionally of a surfeit of lampreys but possibly of a heart attack, the throne of England awaited a prompt claimant. First to move was Matilda's cousin Stephen of Blois (William the Conqueror's grandson) who seized his chance and sailed for England, where he charmed his way to the throne.

His coronation in 1135 split the barons: those with English lands looked to Stephen as the man of the moment; those with lands in France looked to Matilda. Civil war began.

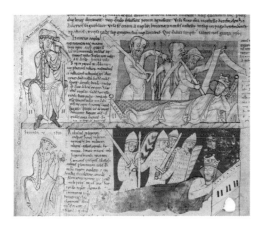

THE KING'S ROYAL NIGHTMARE

In this picture of Henry I's 'nightmare' (1130), people of all classes appear in the king's dream to protest against high taxes. 'His sleep was heavy and marked by much snoring,' reported William of Malmesbury.

HENRY MOURNS

Here Henry I laments the loss of three of his children, including his heir William, in the White Ship *(1120). His nephew Stephen did not sail as planned. He complained of illness – and so survived.*

'Each of his triumphs only made him worry lest he lose what he had gained; therefore though he seemed to be the most fortunate of kings, he was in truth the most miserable.'

Henry of Huntingdon, chronicler, on Henry I

CIVIL WAR

BRAVE, AFFABLE, POPULAR but unreliable – Stephen lacked the single-minded masterfulness of his grandfather, William the Conqueror, and uncles and so failed to stamp his authority swiftly. Nobles took sides and when, in 1139, Empress Matilda landed at Arundel to claim her throne, the anarchy that followed lasted until 1154. Neither side ever summoned the strength for outright victory in a small-scale but vicious civil war.

Royal authority was flouted as roving bands of baronial troops burned and looted towns. The chronicles of the time paint a fearful picture of a land ransacked by 'wicked men' and detail the tortures inflicted on anyone thought to have any treasures or secrets worth extracting under duress: hanging by the thumbs or by the head, having knotted ropes tied around the head and twisted, being locked up in dismal cells with horrid creatures of all kinds – 'adders and snakes and toads'. If the histories are to be believed, many thousands were killed by torture or starvation. Such were the horrors of medieval anarchy.

Yet despite such lawlessness, much of the system held. Taxes were paid, courts met, trade staggered on. Matilda sailed from England in 1148, leaving her son Henry to continue the fight. In the end Stephen (whose own son Eustace predeceased him) accepted Henry as his heir. It was a relief to all.

Wide-ranging in talents and interests, celebrated for his physical energy and terrifying rages, Henry II was a figure of European stature, as was his formidable queen, Eleanor of Aquitaine. Reigning from 1154 to 1189, Henry was first of the Angevin or Plantagenet kings, named after the sprig of broom (*planta genista*) worn by his father, Geoffrey of Anjou. The young king's empire – England, Wales, Ireland, Normandy, Anjou, Brittany and Aquitaine – far surpassed that of previous English kings. When he was not quarrelling with family, friends or the Church, Henry drove through a radical restructuring of the English legal system – his most lasting legacy.

THE NEARLY QUEEN

Matilda failed to become England's queen, but was mother to Henry II, first of the Plantagenet kings.

CHRONICLER OF CIVIL WAR

Born around 1143 and raised from boyhood in Malmesbury Abbey, Somerset, William of Malmesbury was a monastic librarian turned historian. He knew many great men of the time, including Roger of Salisbury and Robert of Gloucester (Matilda's half-brother and ally in the civil war).

'Every rich man built his castle ...'

Castle Rising in Norfolk was one of many castles built during the civil wars and, as its name suggests, it stands on an immense earth rampart some 20 metres (66 feet) high. Its first owner was William de Albini, Earl of Sussex, who married Henry I's widow.

'Mild and soft ...'

King Stephen with a falcon, from a 14th-century manuscript. The Anglo-Saxon Chronicle lambasts lawless barons who took advantage of the 'mild and soft' king's weakness: 'they oppressed the wretched people ... and that lasted the nineteen years while Stephen was king and it was always going from bad to worse.'

'[Stephen] was a man of activity, but imprudent; strenuous in war; of great mind in attempting works of difficulty; mild and compassionate to his enemies and affable to all. Kind as far as promise went, but sure to disappoint in its truth and execution.' William of Malmesbury

21

A GODLY REALM

SUNSET SILHOUETTE

The massive silhouette of Durham Cathedral, the foundations of which were laid in 1093 as a shrine for the body of St Cuthbert.

THE WORK OF THIRTY YEARS

An illuminated letter from the Winchester Bible, which was created over a period of 30 years for Henry of Blois (1129–71), Bishop of Winchester and brother of King Stephen.

THE CHRISTIANITY that came to Britain in Roman times lingered in Celtic areas of the north and west, including Wales and Ireland, producing such 4th-century missionary saints as Ninian, Illtud and Patrick. Celtic monks set up isolated monasteries on offshore islands like Iona, where Columba landed from Ireland (563), and Lindisfarne, founded off the coast of Northumbria by Aidan (635). The job of converting pagan Saxons was begun by missionaries from Rome, starting with Augustine (597) and Christianity flourished, thanks to godly English kings such as Alfred the Great. From the fusion of Roman, Celtic and Saxon traditions evolved a renowned literate Christian culture that had created such glorious masterpieces as the Book of Kells and the Lindisfarne Gospels.

In 1066, Christian England still had many traces of its old Celtic, Saxon and Norse beliefs and customs. The Norman Conquest hit it full force with the vigour of monastic life flourishing in continental Europe. Renewed intellectual and spiritual energy inspired a rush of religious building, as many impressive stone churches, abbeys and cathedrals soared heavenwards.

Senior churchmen rivalled powerful nobles in medieval times: the Pope in Rome could even rebuke a king. Meanwhile, the humble priest preached to his flock, using Latin, the universal language of the medieval Roman Church. This was the golden age of the huge medieval monasteries, run by four main orders (Benedictines, Cluniacs, Cistercians and Carthusians), whose foundations endured until their decay and dissolution by Henry VIII in the 1500s.

CASTLE AND CATHEDRAL

This view of the site of Old Sarum, an ancient settlement outside Salisbury, shows the foundations of the old Norman castle (right) and cathedral. In 1220, Bishop Richard Poore abandoned the 'waterless hill-fort' and started to build a new cathedral in the valley below.

MONKS AND MONASTERIES

MONASTIC VINTAGE

St Benedict told monks: 'to drink temperately and not to satiety, for wine maketh even the wise fall away'. Some monasteries became famous for their winemaking, and wine was celebrated in book art.

FOUNTAINS ABBEY

Fountains Abbey, near Ripon in Yorkshire, became the foremost Cistercian monastery in England. Founded in 1132, Fountains was the North's largest single producer of wool.

LARGE ABBEYS WERE as busy as small towns – though less noisy – and many owned numerous estates. In Suffolk, Bury St Edmunds had 170 manors; Fountains Abbey, Yorkshire, all or part of 150. A community of 60 monks might run what was by medieval standards a large and hugely profitable business.

Directing a monastic community was the abbot (or abbess in a convent of nuns), assisted by the prior. Each day, sometime between midnight and 3 a.m., a bell roused sleeping monks from their dormitory for the night office (Mattins), the first in a continuous series of services and prayers delivered in chant-like plainsong. Soon after Mattins came Lauds, followed by Prime (around dawn), Terce, Sext (at midday), None, Vespers and Compline (at dusk) before bed.

Monasteries – guardians of priceless libraries – were often the only providers of education for children. Monks copied precious books by hand in the centuries before printing – their careful script embellished by skilled artists with richly coloured 'illuminations'.

'The youthful monk is bidden to wash his hands before his meals … He is not to seize upon the vegetables; nor to use his own spoon in the common dish; nor to lean upon the table; nor to cut or dirty the table cloth.'

From the 'Babees Book' for the instruction of novices at Barnwell

Mealtimes in the refectory were for the most part silent, though one monk or nun might read aloud while the rest ate. Nuns at Syon Abbey, Middlesex, used sign language to replace speech: to ask for fish they moved the hand sideways 'in the manere of a fissh tail'; for mustard, a sister rubbed her nose with her right hand. The monkish diet was frugal. Meat was eaten only by the sick, and meals consisted mainly of bread, eggs, a little wine, and vegetables. Cooks were ingenious in giving variety to this rather monotonous fare. Hygiene was a significant part of monastic life, and before he entered the refectory, a monk paused to wash his hands outside the door. This was an important routine, at a time when people ate mainly with the fingers.

Lay brothers supplied most of the muscle for the monastery's manual work, while the monks prayed or studied. Churchmen managed their estates with close interest on day-to-day business, as we know from surviving letters. Around 1100, Herbert de Losinga, first Bishop of Norwich, wrote a scolding letter to William the Monk, one of his officials. The Bishop was upset about the wilful uprooting of woodland, and in his letter he complained that he had appointed William as 'guardian, not uprooter of that wood [Thorpe Wood]'. The Bishop points out that it is his wish to give money, not wood, to the poor people of Norwich on his next visit. Whether

MONKISH SCHOLAR
Medieval monasteries were centres of learning. This 12th-century illustration shows the writer Eadwine, a monk at Canterbury.

this was inspired by an episcopal desire to protect the environment, or by a commercial instinct that the wood should be sold rather than simply given away, remains a matter of conjecture

CATHEDRALS AND CHURCHES

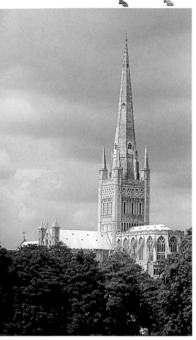

NORWICH CATHEDRAL

Begun in 1096, Norwich Cathedral was finally consecrated in 1278. Constructed mainly from Normandy's Caen stone, the 96-metre (315-foot) spire is second in height only to that of Salisbury Cathedral.

THE NORMANS BUILT as nobody in Britain since Roman times, to glorify God and underline their own supremacy. William the Conqueror began at once, founding his first English abbey on the victory site at Battle. Then he shook up England's Church as he had its government, setting energetic Normans to update an institution whose venerated Saxon saints they thought 'rustic', and learned abbots 'uncultured idiots'.

Lanfranc, first Norman Archbishop of Canterbury, organized dioceses and developed Church law courts. He also tried, less successfully, to make a priest's blessing necessary for legal marriage – and to make priests celibate.

Church-building enthusiastically, Normans first employed the monumental Romanesque style of huge stone columns and heavy, rounded arches. Mirroring the builders' own strength, energy, confidence and endurance, the grandest examples are the cathedrals at Durham, Ely, Norwich, Gloucester, Winchester, and Tewkesbury Abbey, with aisles, galleries and arcades flanking immensely long naves.

Saxons provided the labour but stonemasons and craftsmen came from Normandy, organized by monks such as Bishop Gundulf, who rebuilt Rochester's cathedral and put up its castle.

Worldly bishops wielded power like barons (and some rode to battle with them), but they held the Church's lands from the king, swearing fealty (allegiance) and providing fighting men in return. And good churchman though he was, William I insisted on being master in his new realm. No pope was to be recognized in England without the king's sanction – a regal stance imitated by later kings who showed defiance or indifference to Rome.

Henry I welcomed Cistercian monks to England, where they raised sheep at Rievaulx and Fountains abbeys in Yorkshire. Dominican friars arrived in 1221; Franciscans three years later. By 1300 there were over 5,000 friars in England, though by Chaucer's time their reputation had sunk somewhat, for Chaucer's Friar is 'a wantowne and a merye', dishing out forgiveness for sins in return for cash.

CATHEDRAL CURIOSITIES

England's oldest surviving clock, dating from 1386, is at Salisbury Cathedral. In the cathedral cloisters, which are the largest in England, can be seen this simple cat, cut into the stone.

ELY'S SOARING LANTERN

Ely Cathedral's unique feature is the octagon, with its 200-tonne wooden lantern soaring above. An engineering masterpiece conceived by the cathedral's brilliant monk-administrator, Alan de Walsingham, it replaced the old tower that collapsed in 1322.

CHRISTMAS BATH FOR CANTERBURY MONKS

'On the vigil of Thomas the apostle, if it be not a Sunday, **the brethren shall be shaved and let those who will take a bath,** in such wise that all shall have taken it two days before Christmas Day ... The brethren ... when shaved, shall **enter the bathing place as directed, and letting down the curtain** that hangs before them they shall **sit in silence in the bath** ... When he has finished washing himself, **he shall not stay longer for pleasure but shall rise and dress** and put on his shoes.'

From the *Monastic Constitutions of Lanfranc*, Archbishop of Canterbury, 1070–89

WESTMINSTER ABBEY

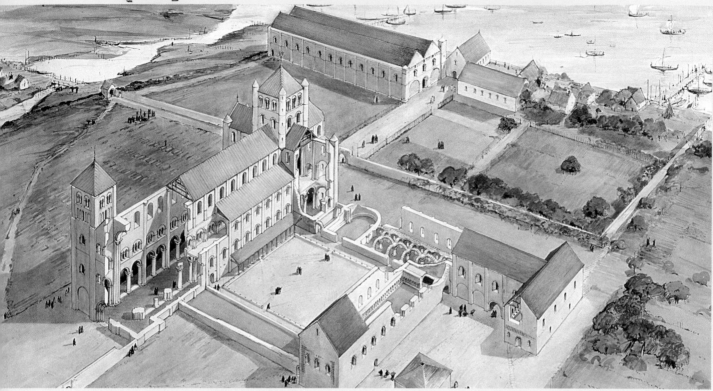

WHERE THE CONQUEROR WAS CROWNED

An artist's view of Westminster Abbey in 1100. The Thames of Saxon and Norman times was a busy waterway serving London and its great abbey church.

REPOSE OF KINGS
Funeral effigy of King Henry III, who rebuilt the abbey and was buried in the Chapel of Edward the Confessor. The chapel's other royal tombs are those of Edward I, Richard II, Edward III and Henry V.

HOW OLD IS WESTMINSTER ABBEY? There is no easy answer to the question posed by most visitors to this famous landmark. Legend places it back in the 7th century, to a Saxon church on the 'Isle of Thorns' – the old name for Westminster.

Around 960, St Dunstan, Bishop of London, set up a group of monks at Westminster. They followed the Benedictine Rule and founded a school that survived long after the abbey was emptied of its monks at the Reformation in the 1500s. In 1065, King Edward the Confessor built a church beside the abbey, near his palace. He was buried there – and William I was later crowned there in 1066.

Most of the surviving abbey was built for Henry III between 1245 and 1272, under the eye of three master masons: Henry de Reyns, John of Gloucester and Robert of Beverley. The Chapter House was completed in 1253 and in 1268 the abbey gained one of its finest treasures, the Cosmati pavement in front of the altar.

SEAT OF MAJESTY

Since 1308 all English sovereigns have been crowned in the Coronation Chair – except three: Edward V, Edward VIII (who abdicated in 1936) and, it appears, Mary I (1553–58).

It took 200 more years (up to 1517) to finish the nave. Although much of the outside of London's great abbey looks little different today from the 1500s, the inside was transformed after the Reformation. The 13th-century quire stalls, where monks worshipped day and night, were removed in the late 18th century.

The Coronation Chair, once gilded and delicately moulded, was left unprotected for many years and boys from Westminster School were not alone in taking a chance to carve their names into history! The chair, ordered by Edward I to hold the Stone of Scone (the so-called Stone of Destiny on which Scottish kings were crowned) captured from the Scots, now stands Stone-less, since the trophy was returned to Scotland in 1996.

CHAPTER HOUSE

The Chapter House, housing royal records, escaped the ravages of the dissolution of the monasteries. It was originally the meeting place for the monks, presided over by their abbot.

THE COSMOS IN MARBLE

Coloured marble chips, inlaid into a plain marble ground, produce the pictures of the Cosmati pavement, named after the Italian family who developed the technique. They depict the world according to the Ptolemaic system, accepted in the Middle Ages as explaining the workings of the universe.

CRUSADERS AND PILGRIMS

PILGRIMS HAD SPECIAL STATUS in medieval times, when visits to holy places combined a holiday with religious rewards. The great prize was a visit to Jerusalem which was seen by believers as the centre of the universe. Although Muslim Arabs had occupied Palestine since 638, Christians had been free to travel there and back. Things changed with a Seljuk Turk victory at the Battle of Manzikert in 1071. Unlike the Arabs, the Seljuk Turks were hostile to Christian pilgrims.

In 1095, Pope Urban II called on Christian warriors to march east and reopen the way to the Holy Land. Rallying enthusiastically to the cause, European kings and knights set off on the First Crusade in 1096. Seven more expeditions followed over the next 300 years. None of them succeeded, but the campaigns of the cross had a lasting effect on Europe. Most famous of English crusaders was King Richard I, the Lionheart, who jointly led the Third Crusade.

WEST CHARGES EAST

Western knights sweated in chain-mail armour during clashes with more lightly equipped Muslim cavalry in the Holy Land.

Crusaders and pilgrims faced testing journeys and for most Jerusalem was a distant dream. Closer to home were the shrines of popular saints. Famous pilgrim centres included those of the Virgin Mary at Walsingham in Norfolk and the saintly shrines of: Bury St Edmunds (Edmund the Martyr, died 869); Worcester (Oswald, died 992, and Wulfstan, died 1095); Ely (Etheldreda, died 679); Durham (Cuthbert, died 687); Ripon (Wilfred, died 709); and of course Canterbury (Thomas Becket, died 1170).

Pilgrims put up at roadside inns, where fresh horses were available for those who could afford their hire. William Langland gives us a verse picture of a typical pilgrim in *Piers Plowman, c.* 1370.

> *In pilgrim's dress apparelled, he had a staff*
> *in his hand,*
> *Bound with broad list like bindweed*
> *twisted round it,*
> *A bowl and bag he bare at his side,*
> *And on his hat a hundred flasks of lead ...*

ONWARD CHRISTIAN SOLDIERS

The crusades drew soldiers, idealists, religious fanatics, adventurers and opportunists from across Europe. As William of Malmesbury drily observed in the early 1100s, to go on crusade, 'The Welshman left his hunting; the Scot his fellowship with vermin; the Dane his drinking party; the Norwegian his raw fish ... **The road was too narrow for the passengers,** the path too confined for the travellers, **so thickly were they thronged with endless multitudes.** The number surpassed all human imagination.'

Pilgrim tokens included small lead phials of holy water, as well as crosses and scallop shells. Saints were the celebrities of the Middle Ages and collectors snapped up every relic offered – blood and bone, genuine and false.

TAKING SHIP FOR A HOLY WAR
Crusaders embarking for the East were unsure of ever seeing their native lands again.

CHESTER'S PILGRIM
This carved wooden figure of a pilgrim can be seen in the quire of Chester Cathedral.

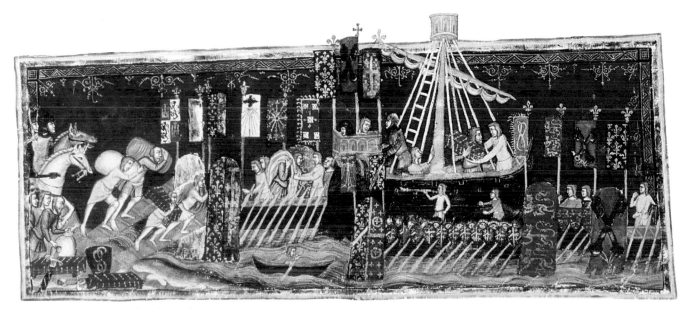

Murder in the Cathedral

MURDER SCENE
The Altar of the Sword's Point in Canterbury Cathedral stands near the spot where Becket was killed. The crown of Becket's head, hacked off by a sword, was kept in the Corona Chapel.

THE MURDER OF THOMAS BECKET in 1170 caused a sensation in England and throughout Europe.

Born in 1118, the son of a London merchant, Becket had climbed to the top of the Church's career ladder, though it was his talent as a 'fixer' that recommended him to King Henry II. A favoured adviser, he helped to increase royal power over the Church's affairs (and wealth) and in 1161, the king repaid Becket by appointing him as Archbishop of Canterbury.

Becket then made a dramatic about-face and began a dogged opposition to the king taking over the privileges of the Church. Matters came to a head in 1163 when the archbishop was charged with treason and had to flee abroad for seven years. In June 1170, a half-hearted compromise enabled Becket's return to defend his Church, and to make sure it was not overwhelmed by the power of the state. But now Becket found himself at odds with the clergy as well as the court, and even sacked the prior at Canterbury.

STORYTELLERS ON THE ROAD

Geoffrey Chaucer used the pilgrimage to Thomas Becket's shrine as the vehicle for his *Canterbury Tales*. Three of his storytelling travellers are shown here: the Knight, the Wife of Bath and the Parson. Chaucer (c.1340–1400) was the first English writer to be buried in Westminster Abbey and the first poet in Poets' Corner.

Henry's wrath came to the boil after he was told (while in France) that Becket was possibly raising a private army in Kent. He raged at his courtiers, asking why a low-born clerk was allowed to treat a king with such contempt. 'Who will rid me of this turbulent priest?'

Four knights took royal wrath as regal command, sailed to England and confronted Becket in Canterbury Cathedral on 29 December. Becket resisted arrest and they drew swords. A monk (Edward Grim) tried to defend Becket, later telling how the 'wicked knight ... leapt upon him suddenly and wounded this lamb, who was sacrificed to God, on the head, cutting off the top of the crown ... and by the same blow he wounded the arm of him who tells this.' Beaten to the floor, Becket died bloodily. The four knights and a fifth man, a 'clerk' according to Grim, then fled.

Becket was acclaimed a martyr. Canterbury's citizens brought bottles and scooped up blood from the stones or dipped shreds of clothing into it. Guilt-ridden and contrite, King Henry came to Canterbury in 1174 to walk barefoot and be scourged by monks at Becket's tomb. Soon, the shrine was bringing wealth to the city. Lodging-house business boomed as pilgrims thronged to the scene of the crime: the Chequer of Hope in Mercery Lane could sleep 600 guests though it had only 100 (very large) beds!

RECONSTRUCTION OF CRIME SCENE

This reconstruction of a medieval painting shows the four knights attacking the archbishop. The original (now defaced) can be seen at the tomb of King Henry IV in Canterbury Cathedral.

SWORD AND STONE

Harlech Castle was one of Edward I's Welsh fortresses, built 1283–89. Under the direction of Master James of St George, 950 men were at times employed on the building work.

DAVID AND GOLIATH

A chain-mailed Norman knight towers above a defiant, but less well-armoured, opponent.

MEDIEVAL ENGLAND was ruled by the sword as well as the Bible. The king let out lands (fiefs) to the Church and to lords (barons) who in turn let out portions of land to warrior-knights. The barons were also military commanders, with forces that could rival the king's in size. Castles built by William the Conqueror and his successors, notably Edward I, were far more than garrison bases. They were centres of government, statements of intent and symbols of power.

In Norman England there were around 3,000 or more knights (roughly 100 knights for every baron). They were fighting men, trained for combat in armour on horseback, with a range of fearsome weapons. Knights were bound to their lord by loyalty and military service in exchange for his land, which he in turn let out to peasants who farmed it. Each knight had to supply a specified number of soldiers. This military bond held medieval government together. If the bond broke, civil war and anarchy threatened.

No baron was supposed to build a castle without the king's consent. The first Norman castles were forts made of wood, erected after the Conquest of 1066 and later enlarged and strengthened. Great stone towers or keeps rose up within an outer curtain wall, interspersed with towers and protected by a massive gatehouse. Across the land the castles stood, as many endure today. Sword and stone – these were the power-symbols of medieval England.

KNIGHTS ON HORSEBACK

Thundering ponderously into battle, the mounted knight was the most powerful strike weapon of medieval England.

35

KING V. BARONS

If KING RICHARD I is remembered for crusading during long absences from England, his brother John is recalled for upsetting the barons, losing the crown jewels in the Wash, and putting his seal to Magna Carta.

King John's tomb in Gloucester Cathedral. Magna Carta is, ironically, his lasting monument.

John was a sadly unsuccessful king. In 1204 he lost Normandy to France, and in 1205 he crossed the Pope by refusing to accept Stephen Langton as Archbishop of Canterbury. He enraged his barons by taking not only their taxes, but the land of any who refused to pay. By 1213 they determined to oppose him.

Faced with humiliating invasion from France, John submitted to the Pope in return for money. But not even this abject surrender could save him. Defeat in Normandy had ended all chance of his barons recouping lost lands and revenue there, so the disgruntled lords instead demanded a charter setting out their feudal rights. John stalled, even taking a crusader's oath to win the Church's favour (he had no intention of actually heading for the East), but no matter how hard he wriggled, he was hooked. The barons

HISTORY ON CALFSKIN

Magna Carta – 'the Great Charter' – was written on vellum, a fine parchment of calfskin. The 'Salisbury exemplification' was one of at least 13 copies sent around the country. Four survive – this one at Salisbury, one at Lincoln, and two in the British Library. The seal of King John, similar to the one illustrated here, was attached to authenticate each exemplification of Magna Carta.

threatened civil war, London sided with them, and in 1215 – after secret talks involving Archbishop Langton and the king's adviser William Marshal, Earl of Pembroke – a deal was struck.

Barons and monarch met at Runnymede by the Thames, near Windsor. The terms were read out, probably by Langton. John declared his agreement, and his seal was attached to the document. Within days he asked the Pope to annul it and the Pope duly declared Magna Carta to be 'as unlawful and unjust as it is base and shameful'. But there was no going back.

Civil war erupted. After aimless raids and losing his baggage train in the soft sands of the Wash, John moved south to fight an invading French army. His end was unheroic, dying at Newark of dysentery.

Bad King John was succeeded by the boy-king Henry III – and Magna Carta took on new significance. As reluctant guardian of the realm, William Marshal reissued Magna Carta in the nine-year-old king's name: the document was not going to be consigned to the rubbish tip. This won over the barons, and the French prudently withdrew. The Crown was saved. The course of constitutional history – and not just in England alone – was altered for ever. Kings were henceforth expected to uphold the rights of the Church and the barons. Magna Carta has been seen as a landmark in the growth of constitutional government, even though its 63 articles said little about the rights and freedoms of ordinary people.

THE BARONS
RIDE FORTH

John's demand for money to fight wars which he then lost made him doubly unpopular with the English barons.

RUNNYMEDE RIGHTS – EXTRACTS FROM MAGNA CARTA

'The English church shall be free and shall have her rights undiminished and her liberties unimpaired.'
(Section 1)

'We decree and grant that **all cities, boroughs, towns and ports shall have their liberties and free customs.'**
(Section 13)

'Let there be **one measure of wine** throughout our kingdom, and **one measure of ale, and one of corn … and one width of cloth.** Let it be the same with weights as with measures.'
(Section 35)

'No free man shall be taken or imprisoned … except by the lawful judgement of his peers or by the law of the land.'
(Section 39)

'Magna Carta is the greatest constitutional document of all times – the foundation of the freedom of the individual against the arbitrary authority of the despot.'

Lord Denning, Master of the Rolls, 1965

KNIGHTS IN ARMOUR

NORMAN KNIGHTS were skilled horsemen on the battlefield and in the hunting forest. Their warhorse was the destrier, ridden high in the saddle by a warrior clad in a hauberk, a knee-length shirt of chain mail. On his head sat a conical metal helmet, worn over a padded head-piece, and a mail hood called a coif. His shield was kite-shaped, with later versions being smaller for easier control on horseback.

KNIGHTLY CONQUEROR
An illustration from about 1321 shows William the Conqueror decked out in the trappings of a contemporary knight.

Mounted knights rode straight-legged with stirrups, giving a firm seat for control of a long lance. Chain mail remained the most common body armour until the 1300s, when plate armour in sections was developed to cover all parts of the body, including the hands. Plate armour, skilfully shaped to allow movement, was secured with leather straps. Helmets, progressively ornate, could be open-faced or fitted with hinged visors. Not only riders but horses too were armoured, wearing metal chanfrons for head protection as well as decorated harnesses.

The knight fought with knightly weapons: axe, hammer, mace, lance and sword. Lowly men-at-arms might carry a sword and wear a helmet, but wore little armour.

By the 13th century only sons of noble families were admitted to the orders of knighthood. To be worthy of his rank, a knight was expected to observe a strict code of honour and virtue – the code of chivalry. Training and equipping a knight became prolonged and costly; boys not born to wealth were inevitably excluded.

A knight was expected to give up his time to serve his feudal lord – 40 days a year for training or guarding castles, longer in time of war. He had to provide his own horses too. The ideal was three horses: one for fighting, one for riding, one for

carrying the baggage. The knight was
also expected to live up to the ideals of
chivalry, both the romantic ideals of the
troubadours' ballads and the religious
ideals of the Church, which added the
all-night vigil to the knight-making ceremony of being 'dubbed' – touched on the
shoulders with a sword. Few could have
lived up to the model of Chaucer's
'perfect gentle knight' who had travelled
far, seen much and earned his spurs: 'and
though so much distinguished, he was
wise and in his bearing modest as a maid.'

The knight was not invincible. An arrow
or crossbow could send him crashing to
earth (often by disabling his horse). On
foot he might meet a swift and bloody
end at the hands of knife- or pitchfork-
wielding peasants. But mounted and
charging at a steady pace suited to his
heavy warhorse – rather than a mad
gallop – he was a sight to strike awe and
terror into his foes.

KNIGHTLY KIT
*A window in Tewkesbury
Abbey, Gloucestershire, shows
14th-century knights in plate
armour, with heraldic surcoats
or 'coats of arms'.*

'*To protect the Church, to fight against treachery, to
reverence the priesthood, to fend off injustice from
the poor, to make peace in our own province, to shed
blood for your brethren and, if needs must, lay down
your life.*'

John of Salisbury (c. 1115–80), describing the duties of a knight, in Polycraticus

39

ENGLAND AND WALES

WILLIAM THE CONQUEROR declared himself 'lord of Wales' in 1071. Along the English border, in lands known as the Marches, the Normans set up three earldoms under the control of so-called Marcher lords: Chester, Shrewsbury and Hereford. Marcher lords soon expanded westward into Wales, building castles as they went. By 1092 Roger Montgomery, Earl of Shrewsbury, had pressed west to Cardigan Bay. In the 1100s the Clares expanded from their Chepstow base, building at least nine castles, including the fortress at Cardigan that fell to fiery Welsh rebellion in the mid-1100s.

Secure in their uplands, Welsh princes of Gwynedd resisted the steady English (or Norman) pressure – notably Llywelyn ap Iorwerth ('the Great') whose grandson, Llywelyn ap Gruffydd ('the Last'), was recognized as Prince of Wales in 1240. Though Llywelyn ap Gruffydd had acknowledged Henry III as overlord, he refused to kneel to the new English king, Edward I. It cost him his crown. Edward declared war, invading North Wales while other forces raised by the Marcher lords attacked the south and centre. Edward advanced along the coast and up the rivers, building castles where

THE FIRST ENGLISH PRINCE OF WALES

Edward I's son, born in 1284 in Caernarfon Castle, was – according to tradition – presented as a baby to the Welsh as their prince. The young Edward was formally created Prince of Wales in 1301.

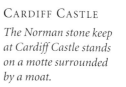

CARDIFF CASTLE

The Norman stone keep at Cardiff Castle stands on a motte surrounded by a moat.

they would dominate the valleys. After Llywelyn's death in a skirmish in 1282, Wales lacked a unifying leader and Edward's victory was assured.

Having created his eldest son Prince of Wales in 1301, Edward left the Marcher lords their lands and Owen Glyndwr's guerrilla uprising of 1400 failed to break the English grip on Wales. Though he captured some castles (only to lose them again), Glyndwr never solved the strategic problem posed by such immense forts, on sites that could be resupplied by sea or river. In 1404 a garrison of only 28 men held Caernarfon Castle against him. The Welsh uprising finally fizzled out under relentless onslaught by Prince Henry, later Henry V. Glyndwr vanished into Welsh folktale. By the 1500s, Wales had become formally part of the Tudor realm.

PINNED TO THE SADDLE

Gerald the Welshman (Giraldus Cambrensis c. 1146 – c. 1220) describes impressive Welsh archery:

'The Welsh ... penetrated with their arrows the oaken portal of the tower, which was four fingers thick' (the arrows were left in the gate, as souvenirs of the fight). One soldier, writes Gerald, **'had his hip,** sheathed in armour, **penetrated by an arrow quite to the saddle,** and on turning his horse round, received a similar wound on the opposite hip, **which fixed him on both sides of his seat.'**

GOING TO WAR

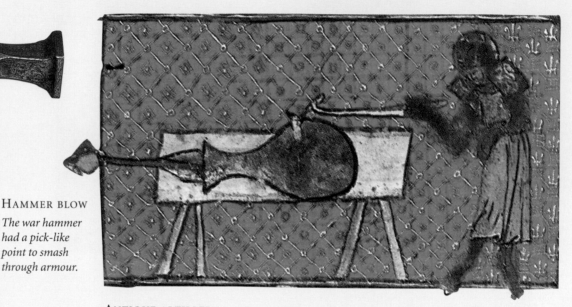

HAMMER BLOW
The war hammer had a pick-like point to smash through armour.

ANTIQUE ARTILLERY
This is the earliest-known illustration of a cannon, 1326, which fired a giant dart – noisily but to no great distance nor with any accuracy.

BATTLES IN THE MIDDLE AGES were mostly small but vicious. Pre-fight courtesies – or insults – might be exchanged between leaders, but after the formalities came the gore. At close quarters, savage hacking and clubbing with swords, axes, maces and other fearsome weapons severed limbs and battered opponents senseless. Not even plate armour offered invulnerability.

A longbow made from yew wood stood about as tall as a man (1.8 metres/6 feet) and needed a pull of about 90 kilograms (200 pounds) to draw back the string. The bow could shoot a 'cloth yard' arrow about 400 metres (440 yards). Fast archers could fire at a rate of ten a minute.

At long range, the longbow was supreme. English and Welsh archers felled many French knights during the battles of Poitiers (1356) and Agincourt (1415). Crossbows, wound by a crank-handle, were less popular in England than in mainland Europe.

Giant catapults hurled stones and other missiles at and over castle walls. Battering rams smashed down wooden gates – the weakest point of any castle. To demolish a wall or tower, 'miners' tunnelled under it, setting wooden props which they then burned away with a wood-and-oil fire. During King John's siege of Rochester in 1215, he ordered 'forty bacon pigs of the

> '[Knights deserved] palfreys or riding horses, and pacing war horses … in order that they may be better cheered, there should sound together trumpets, pipes, flutes and horns. There should be poorer horses, with jolting gait, for the riff-raff.'
>
> *Alexander Neckham (d. 1217)*

NORMAN SWORDS

Long swords were swung with both hands. Blades were straight and double-edged.

fattest and least good for eating, to bring fire beneath the tower.' The pigs were despatched, and in due course the tower was undermined and tumbled.

Gunpowder was first tried by English soldiers in 1346, when crude cannon bellowed smoke and stones at the Battle of Crécy. The use of gunpowder spelt the end for castle walls and knightly armour — though not for another 200 years.

WATERY DEFENCES

Water from a well held the key to a castle's survival under siege, while a moat added an extra line of defence. Bodiam Castle in East Sussex, begun in 1386, was built quickly, to withstand raids rather than prolonged assault.

43

England and Scotland

From 1286, when King Alexander III of Scotland fell to his death over a cliff during a wild storm, Scotland was set on a path of conflict with England – and legends were created.

England's strongman Edward I planned to unite the two kingdoms by marrying his son to the dead Alexander's granddaughter. But the little child-queen, Margaret (the 'Maid of Norway'), died in Orkney after her sea voyage from Norway. Scotland was left in confusion, with no fewer than 14 claimants to the throne. Edward promptly appointed John Balliol as Scotland's king – and England's vassal.

Scottish pride was outraged. Balliol reluctantly rebelled, met defeat, and quit. Edward put in his own men to rule Scotland and, as a final insult, took away the Stone of Scone, emblem of Scots sovereignty. William Wallace, a firebrand guerrilla leader, then rampaged through Scotland, defeating an English army at the Battle of Stirling Bridge in 1297.

The battle rages
This mural, painted in the 19th century by William Hole, shows Scottish foot soldiers slaying the English cavalry at Bannockburn.

Mud and blood at Bannockburn

An eyewitness, quoted in the Chronicle of Lanercost, describes how '... the great horses of the English **charged the pikes of the Scots, as it were into a dense forest,** there arose a great and **terrible crash of spears** broken and destriers [warhorses] wounded to the death.' The English struggled to retreat across the Bannockburn ditch, where 'many nobles and others fell into it with their horses in the crush ... and **many were never able to extricate themselves.**'

Where Bruce's heart lies
Robert the Bruce died in 1329 and was buried in Dunfermline Abbey, but his embalmed heart was carried by Sir James Douglas on his way to the Holy Land. After Douglas died fighting the Moors in Spain, Bruce's heart was returned to Scotland where it lies buried in Melrose Abbey.

Edward went after Wallace, catching up with the Scots near Falkirk. After tramping around a countryside stripped of food, the impatient English king cried out: 'Thanks be to God, who hitherto hath delivered me from every danger; they need not chase after me, I will go forth and meet them!' Between 10,000 and 15,000 Scots were killed at Falkirk. Wallace escaped but was betrayed, arrested and put to death in London.

After Edward I died in 1307, his incapable son Edward II was no match for Scotland's Robert the Bruce. Edward lost castle after castle, and in 1314 the English were losers at the crucial Battle of Bannockburn. Bannockburn was an immense victory for the Scots, for in earlier defeats their foot-soldiers, armed with unwieldy long spears, had been trampled by English knights and felled by volleys of arrows from longbows. This time the tables were turned. The Scots infantry put the knights to flight, the Welsh archers were scattered by Scottish horsemen, and the English army of some 20,000 became so penned in that it could only give ground. What began as retreat turned into panic-stricken flight. Many English knights were taken prisoner. The English baggage train was also captured, and its contents distributed by the victorious Bruce throughout Scotland. Despite this triumph, Scottish independence was not accepted south of the border until 1328, after Edward II had been thrown off the throne and murdered. Bruce died in 1329 and Edward III launched a new war in 1332, but he failed to subdue the Scots. The seeds of resolution were sown in 1371 when a new dynasty – the Stuarts – took power in Scotland. Meanwhile, cross-border wars continued until 1547.

BRAVEHEART REMEMBERED
This statue of William Wallace is at Bemersyde, near Melrose.

THE HUNDRED YEARS' WAR

WHEN NOT FIGHTING the Welsh or Scots, English kings had business in France. Their landholdings there were substantial, and English kings reserved the right to be French kings too.

The Hundred Years' War lasted from 1337 to 1453, through the reigns of five English kings. Edward III began the conflict by claiming the French throne and he won the two great battles of the first phase: Crécy (1346) and Poitiers (1356). Henry V renewed the war. At around 5,000 men, Henry's army was relatively small but his personal retinue was of kingly size: it included 75 gunners, 12 armourers, 60 grooms, 12 smiths, 124 carpenters,

8 bakers, 13 chaplains and 17 minstrels. The king's campaign rules or 'ordinances of war' issued to all his commanders included the warnings that 'every man be obeisant to his capitene' and that 'no man shall robbe other merchaunt, viteler, surgeon ne barbour.'

At Agincourt (1415), there were eyewitnesses on both sides, watching from the baggage trains. Jean de Waurin was a boy of 15, fighting alongside his father in the French army. He later recalled the carnage as horses wounded by English arrows became uncontrollable and unseated their knights. 'As soon as the English saw this disorder in the vanguard they all entered

CRÉCY, 26 AUGUST 1346

This French account, from the *Chronicles of Jean le Bel*, describes how infantry with pikes (a spear twice as long as the man holding it), and Italian mercenaries were trapped between the English and their own knights. 'The commanders ordered the pikemen and Genoese crossbowmen ... in front of the lords, so as to shoot first at the English ... they were routed ... and **would have taken flight if the companies of chief lords** [the French knights] had not been **so fired with envy** ... that they rushed forward in such disorder that **the pikemen and Genoese were trapped between them and the English.'** In the confusion of falling horses, they **'fell on top of each other like a litter of piglets.'**

OLD AND NEW WEAPONS OF WAR

At Crécy, early cannon were used on the battlefield (foreground), although archers did most damage to the French knights. The man at lower right in this picture is swinging a curved sword called a falchion, designed to break open plate armour.

the fray and throwing down bows and arrows, they took their swords, axes, mallets, billhooks and staves and struck out at the French, many of whom they killed.' Estimates of losses in medieval battles are unreliable, but most historians agree that at Agincourt the French lost between 6,000 and 10,000 men; the English probably little more than 100.

After such a crushing victory, Henry seemed about to fulfil English ambitions by marrying the French king's daughter and siring a son to inherit both kingdoms.

This was not to be. Henry V died in 1422, still a young man, leaving an infant son.

Although he was to survive to manhood, Henry VI was no warrior-king like his father. The English squabbled; the French revived with Joan of Arc and enjoyed their turn to win battles. Not even burning Joan at the stake turned English fortunes. By 1453 the English had lost all the territory they had won – except for Calais, which remained in their hands until 1558.

THE BATTLE COMMENCES AT AGINCOURT

The battlefield at Agincourt was rain-sodden, bogging down armoured knights. In this painting, the armies appear equally matched whereas the English (right) were in fact outnumbered at least four to one.

'So many of the horses were wounded by the English arrows that their riders could not control them, and they caused many more knights to fall.'

Jean de Waurin, recalling the Battle of Agincourt in Collection of Chronicles and Ancient Histories of Great Britain

THE WARS OF THE ROSES

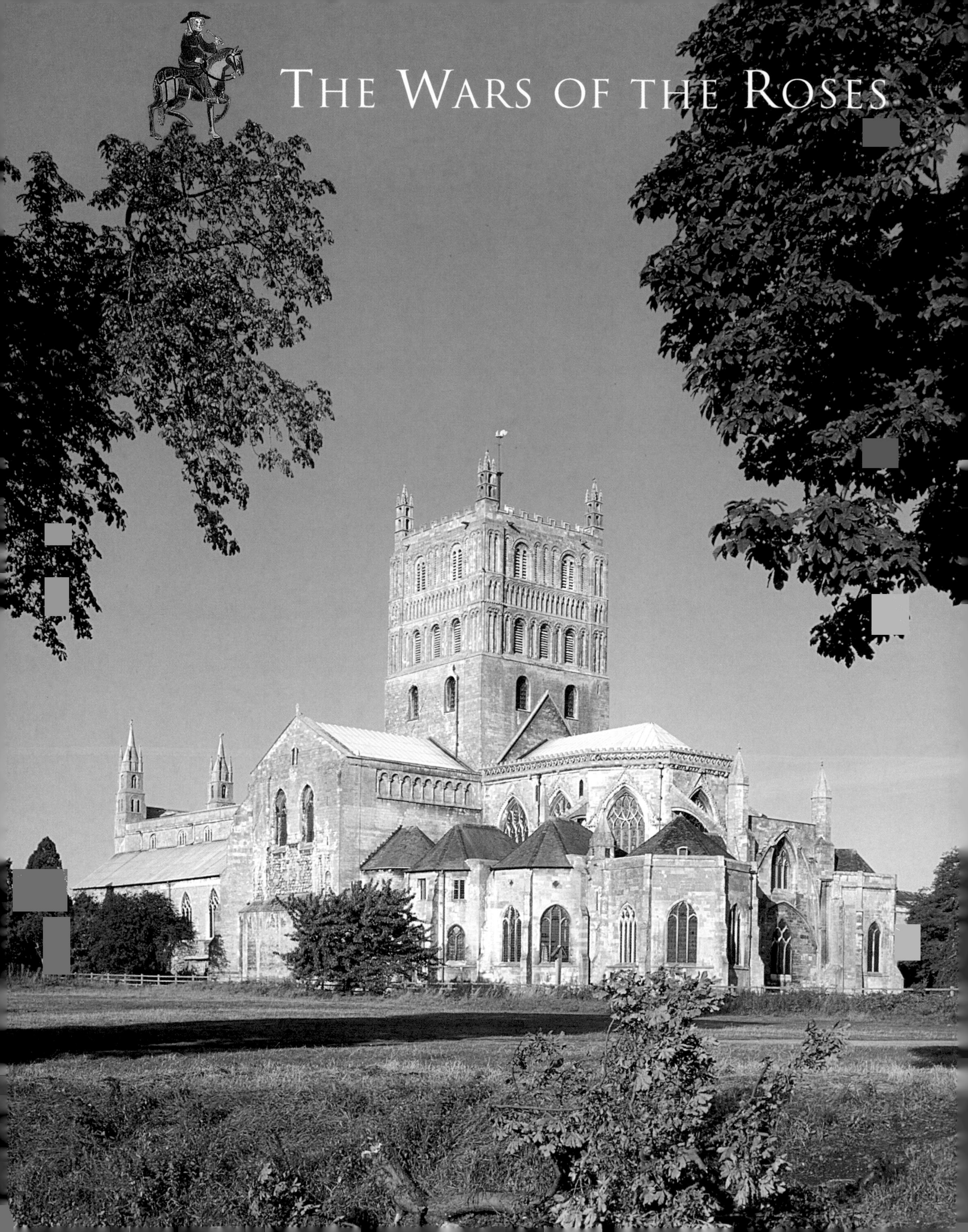

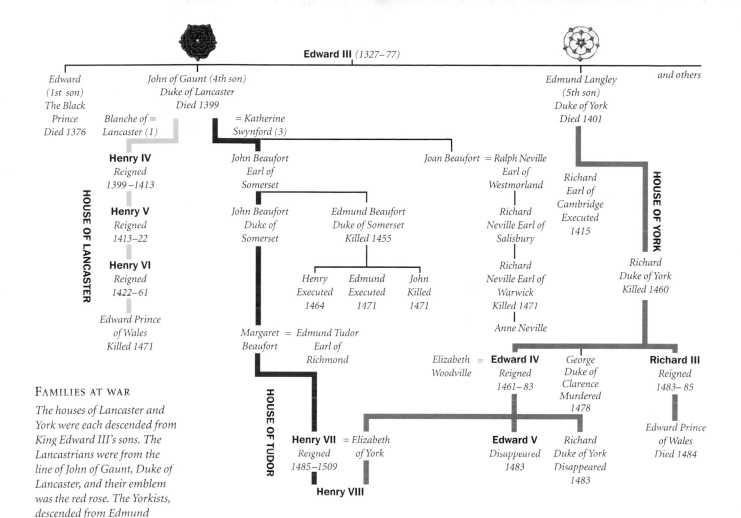

Edward III *(1327–77)*

Edward (1st son) The Black Prince Died 1376

John of Gaunt (4th son) Duke of Lancaster Died 1399

Blanche of = Lancaster (1)

= Katherine Swynford (3)

Edmund Langley (5th son) Duke of York Died 1401

and others

HOUSE OF LANCASTER

Henry IV *Reigned 1399–1413*

Henry V *Reigned 1413–22*

Henry VI *Reigned 1422–61*

Edward Prince of Wales Killed 1471

John Beaufort Earl of Somerset

John Beaufort Duke of Somerset

Edmund Beaufort Duke of Somerset Killed 1455

Henry Executed 1464

Edmund Executed 1471

John Killed 1471

Margaret = Edmund Tudor Beaufort Earl of Richmond

Joan Beaufort = Ralph Neville Earl of Westmorland

Richard Neville Earl of Salisbury

Richard Neville Earl of Warwick Killed 1471

Anne Neville

Richard Earl of Cambridge Executed 1415

Richard Duke of York Killed 1460

HOUSE OF YORK

Elizabeth Woodville = **Edward IV** *Reigned 1461–83*

George Duke of Clarence Murdered 1478

Richard III *Reigned 1483–85*

Edward Prince of Wales Died 1484

HOUSE OF TUDOR

Henry VII *Reigned 1485–1509* = *Elizabeth of York*

Edward V *Disappeared 1483*

Richard Duke of York Disappeared 1483

Henry VIII

FAMILIES AT WAR

The houses of Lancaster and York were each descended from King Edward III's sons. The Lancastrians were from the line of John of Gaunt, Duke of Lancaster, and their emblem was the red rose. The Yorkists, descended from Edmund Langley, Duke of York, adopted the white rose as their badge.

TEWKESBURY ABBEY

The abbey was a Benedictine foundation in the 12th century. One of the abbey doors is reinforced with pieces of armour from the Battle of Tewkesbury (1471), a Yorkist victory in the Wars of the Roses.

THE KINGMAKER'S CALL TO ARMS

This scene at Warwick Castle shows Richard Neville, Earl of Warwick (the 'Kingmaker') calling men to arms. He first supported one side (the Yorkists) but later changed sides – and lost his life.

THE WARS OF THE ROSES fought in England during the 1400s have been portrayed as vicious struggles between gangsterish noble families, with the Crown as the prize and the common people as hapless victims.

The truth about these civil wars is rather more complex. Power did change hands, often with bewildering speed, as fortunes ebbed and flowed, yet English society was, in general, relatively stable and prosperous. The frequent battles were brief, if bloody, and did not lay waste to the countryside. Lordly knights in their steel armour were eager to strike down rivals, but not to destroy the land from which they drew their wealth. Beneath the power-struggle was an evolutionary national process – the working out on home ground of the consequences of a loss of power abroad (in France).

Seen in this light, the Wars of the Roses show England emerging from the long shadow cast by medieval France over the land since the Norman Conquest.

YORK AND LANCASTER

ENGLAND IN THE 1440s looked peaceful and prosperous, yet cracks were showing. Cash and contracts had largely replaced the old feudal obligations. From their castles, nobles ruled like magnates (or gang bosses), and looked to a strong king to command them.

The Lancastrian king Henry VI was bookish and pliable. He was described by one of his priests, John Blakman, as commonly wearing 'shoes, boots, hose, everything of a dark grey colour – for he would have nothing fanciful.' In 1453 this pious monarch suffered a devastating mental breakdown that left him incapable of government. Royal coffers were almost empty, wars in France had been lost, and embittered nobles split into hostile and squabbling factions.

DESCRIPTION OF THE BATTLE OF ST ALBANS, 1455

'The Earl of Warwick [fighting for the Yorkist cause] took his men and **ferociously broke in by the garden sides** between the sign of the Key and the sign of the Chequer in Holywell Street and as soon as they were within the town, **they blew trumpets and set up a shout of "a Warwick, a Warwick, a Warwick"** … At this time the lord of Dorset was sore hurt that he could not walk and was carried home in a cart.'

From a contemporary manuscript held by the Steward to the Abbot of St Albans

Claimants clamoured to succeed what they regarded as a sadly demented king. Richard, Duke of York, claiming descent from John of Gaunt, son of Edward III, had himself declared Protector in March 1454, but then to his dismay saw Henry regain health and wits. Carried away by the taste of power, Richard of York resorted to arms, and defeated his principal rivals at the first battle of the Wars of the Roses, which took place at St Albans in May 1455. The white rose was blossoming.

As Yorkist strength grew, Lancastrians rallied to Henry's indomitable queen, Margaret of Anjou, and in June 1459 they came out fighting to take on the Yorkist army at Bloreheath in the West Midlands. As so often, betrayal played its part when a trusted ally of Richard of York, Sir Andrew Trollope, changed sides. Yorkist forces fell apart and Richard, the would-be king, fled to Ireland.

FORMIDABLE QUEEN

Fiery Margaret of Anjou (1430–82) fought doggedly for the cause of her husband, Henry VI, and their son, Prince Edward.

'On the principal [religious] feasts of the year … he would put on next to his skin a rough hair-shirt.' John Blakman, writing about Henry VI

FIRST CLASH

The first battle at St Albans in May 1455 was trivial – casualties may have been as low as 60 men – but marked the start of the Wars of the Roses.

SIRE OF KINGS

John of Gaunt (1340–99), son of Edward III, was the forefather of several English kings: father of Henry IV, grandfather of Henry V and great-grandfather of Henry VI. The Tudors also traced descent from him.

TROUBLED TIMES

**GALLERY FOR THE HEADS
OF TRAITORS**

York's Micklegate Bar was popular for displaying the heads of dead opponents. The Duke of York's head, adorned with a paper crown, was stuck up for all to see.

DESPITE THE WAR, life went on. The fighting during the Wars of the Roses was largely directed by political, not purely military, considerations. Towns were rarely attacked and the countryside was hardly wasted. This was a struggle between rival landholding families, and neither side wanted to see rich estates go up in flames.

A lord could expect to lose his head if captured after a defeat in battle, but his servants were still expected to set a good table for their master. A 1460 book reminds butlers to 'always cut your lord's bread and see that it be new; and all other bread at the table one day old ere you cut it, all household bread three days old, and trencher bread four days old.' Even during a civil war, tablecloth, towel and napkin should be folded neatly, knives polished and 'your spoon fair washed'.

Back in control after the Battle of Bloreheath, the Lancastrians overplayed their hand – trying not only to confiscate rebels' land but also to dispossess their heirs. Outraged, nobles swung back towards the Yorkist cause.

In July 1460, Richard of York's allies captured King Henry VI himself at the Battle of Northampton. York returned to England, and left nobody in doubt of his wish to be king. But he failed to win sufficient backing and in December that year so disastrously mismanaged his army that it was routed at Wakefield where he himself was killed. His head was struck off and stuck on a pole – a grim warning to others.

Victorious Lancastrians swept south on a tide of savagery – a rarity in these wars – and won a second battle of St Albans in February 1461, after which the victorious Queen Margaret was reunited with Henry VI, who had been brought captive to the battle. But the sack of Stamford, in particular, had so appalled the people of London that they truculently refused to open the city gates to Henry

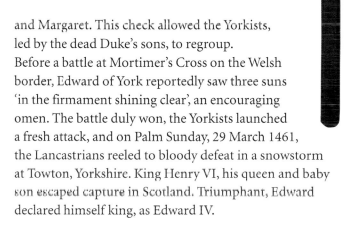

CLOSE ENCOUNTERS

During the Roses battles, superiority shifted from archers to men-at-arms, who fought on foot with long-shafted partisans, halberds and poleaxes. The poleaxe (right) could pierce armour and smash a helmet (below). This sword (left) from about 1450 could well have been used in a Roses battle, where hastily mustered bands of soldiers tried to bludgeon one another in close combat. Sieges were rare. Harlech Castle (shown on page 34) held out for the Lancastrians between 1461 and 1468 – but this was an exception in a war of rapid encounters.

and Margaret. This check allowed the Yorkists, led by the dead Duke's sons, to regroup. Before a battle at Mortimer's Cross on the Welsh border, Edward of York reportedly saw three suns 'in the firmament shining clear', an encouraging omen. The battle duly won, the Yorkists launched a fresh attack, and on Palm Sunday, 29 March 1461, the Lancastrians reeled to bloody defeat in a snowstorm at Towton, Yorkshire. King Henry VI, his queen and baby son escaped capture in Scotland. Triumphant, Edward declared himself king, as Edward IV.

YORK TRIUMPHANT

TALL, HANDSOME, SELF-CONFIDENT, indolent, Edward IV was a ladies' man. 'He pursued with no discrimination the married and the unmarried, the noble and the lowly,' observed one censorious chronicler. But the people liked him, and he evidently had winning ways. 'London merchants seemed flattered to be asked to lend the king money,' an Italian ambassador observed wryly.

~

To cheer a nation at peace, Edward decided to renew England's traditional claim to France, raising a huge sum to finance a new invasion. The adventure lasted less than two months before Edward withdrew – taking cash in return from the relieved French king. Some thought this an astute deal; others considered it less than honourable.

~

The dynastic wars were not over, however. Yorkists had drawn on popular discontent to foment rebellion against Henry VI, whereas the Lancastrians tried international conspiracy. Queen Margaret, experienced in such ploys, remained an implacable foe of York. After Henry VI

BLOODY MEADOW

To this day the name 'Bloody Meadow' testifies to the butchery at the Battle of Tewkesbury, last rite of the Wars of the Roses.

ROYAL SCHEMERS

Though decisive and effective in battle, Edward IV was self-indulgent when out of armour. He was ready to be charmed by his favourite mistress, Jane Shore, and, as it proved, ready to be manipulated by Elizabeth Woodville, who refused to be his lover without also being queen.

LETTER FROM THE FRONT

Sir John Paston, who switched sides to fight for the Lancastrians at Barnet in 1471, wrote home to his mother, Margaret Paston, with news of his brother (also confusingly called Sir John): 'Mother, I recommend me to you, letting you know that, blessed be to God, **my brother John is alive and fareth well and in no peril of death, nevertheless he is hurt with an arrow in his right arm beneath the elbow, and I have sent him a surgeon,** which hath dressed him and he telleth me that **he trusteth that he shall be all whole within right short time.'**

was captured at Clitheroe, Lancashire, in 1465 and imprisoned in the Tower of London, she did not see her husband again, but never ceased plotting to regain the throne.

Edward IV made difficulties for himself by sidelining the ambitious Earl of Warwick. The 'Kingmaker', like other nobles hoping for influence at court, was stung by the meteoric rise of the Woodville family. Elizabeth Woodville had married Edward in 1464 and her family (two sons, five brothers and seven sisters) formed a money-grubbing and envied clique. Disgruntled Warwick threw in his lot with exiles in France. He returned heading a Lancastrian army in September 1470; the Yorkist side splintered, and soon Henry VI was released from the Tower of London. It was Edward's turn to flee abroad. Like it or not, Henry was king again.

But not for long. Edward was back, with additional troops lent by the Duke of Burgundy (himself at war with France), in March 1471. Capturing London, Yorkists again seized the hapless Henry, and defeated the Lancastrians in thick fog at Barnet, where in the confusion Warwick was killed. Queen Margaret and her son Edward, Prince of Wales, landed from France for a final battle, in May 1471, at

Tewkesbury. It was a ruthless Yorkist triumph. Prince Edward was killed, his mother captured, and Henry VI was put to death soon afterwards.

Edward IV seemed secure. He had sons to follow him – and the support of his brother Richard, Duke of Gloucester. But the 40-year-old king's sudden death at Easter 1483 triggered a frantic struggle for control of the 12-year-old Edward V. The Woodvilles and their rival Lord Hastings were no match for a new power in the land. Young King Edward and his brother were swiftly in the hands of their uncle, Richard of Gloucester, now master of the scene.

SCHOLAR-KING WHO LOST HIS HEAD

Henry VI founded Eton College and King's College, Cambridge. When the Lancastrian challenge failed in 1471, he was murdered.

Princes in the Tower

Like a lowering thundercloud, Richard of Gloucester came down on London and the court in mourning. He had ruled the north for his brother Edward IV with brilliant success. Loyal, implacable, scrupulously honest in government yet a cynical manipulator in his own interest, Richard remains one of the most enigmatic personalities in English history.

Prince Edward heard of his father's death at Ludlow Castle, a Yorkist base, and set off for London with a Woodville escort. By the time he got there, he had a new 'minder' – his uncle Richard of Gloucester. For their own protection, Edward and his brother were taken to the Tower, a favourite lodging for royal guests.

Swiftly eliminating both the Woodville clan and the Hastings faction, Richard coolly proclaimed the need to set aside his nephew, not yet crowned Edward V. This was no time for a boy-king to be string-pulled by puppet-master nobles. Civil war must not break out again. England needed firm government, by an experienced Yorkist hand. Church and Parliament anxiously petitioned Richard to take the throne and he graciously accepted.

Richard as King
Richard III, pictured here as a great prince. In his short reign, he proved a capable, strong king.

The Bloody Tower
Richard's nephews were almost certainly murdered here.

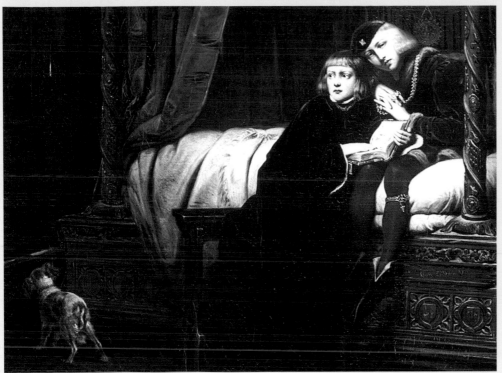

DOOMED PRINCES

The story of the Princes in the Tower is a medieval whodunit. It is more than likely that the boys were murdered, probably by their own side, possibly by their own uncle. The Bloody Tower is the last known resting place of these two young victims of the Wars of the Roses.

RICHARD'S JEWEL?

The so-called Middleham jewel is thought to have belonged to Richard III. This 15th-century gold pendant was found in 1985 near Middleham Castle, Yorkshire, a favourite residence of the king. The craftsmanship is of such exceptional quality that the jewel must have belonged to a very important person.

'... little of stature, ill-featured of limbs, crook-backed, his left shoulder much higher than his right ...'   Thomas More's 1513 account of Richard III

The presence of any royal rival was a constant threat to Richard who, to lessen the danger, had his brother's sons declared illegitimate. Richard III's reign began officially on 26 June 1483.

Richard used no overt military force to win the throne but, having dealt with the Woodvilles and their friends, it is generally assumed that he then ordered the murder of his nephews. Thomas More, writing in 1513 as a Tudor propagandist, declared that the boys were smothered and then buried under a staircase. More left us the familiar picture of the villain Richard III, later adopted by William Shakespeare. There is no mention of obvious deformities in accounts by those who knew King Richard. The Tudor antiquary John Stow (1525–1605) spoke with old men who recalled him as 'comely enough, only of low stature'.

King Edward's sons – glimpsed from time to time – were last seen in the late summer of 1483. Persistent legend places the two princes in the Bloody Tower, where it is said they were murdered. Bones found in a Tower staircase in 1674 may or may not be theirs. What happened to the Princes in the Tower remains a mystery. There is little doubt that they died young – but at whose hand, and on whose orders, remains the subject of debate between pro-Richard and anti-Richard historians.

Richard cannot escape being the chief suspect in this royal murder mystery, but there are others. Henry Tudor, for one, waiting in France and soon to make his bid for the Crown, had an obvious motive for wanting the Yorkist princes out of the way. For his brief reign, Richard remained insecure, always looking over his shoulder.

CROWN CHANGES HANDS

MIDDLEHAM CASTLE

It was here in Yorkshire that Richard III spent most of his childhood and after his marriage in 1472 it was his favourite residence in the north.

RICHARD III'S POWER-BASE – unusually for a medieval king – was in the north. Of the great southern lords, only the Howards of Norfolk stood by him at the end. Even before the close of 1483, he had to quell a revolt by his former ally, the Duke of Buckingham. Then in April 1484, King Richard lost his son and heir through illness, and in March 1485 his queen.

The way lay invitingly open for a challenger – and it came from a somewhat unexpected quarter. Henry V's widow,

Catherine of Valois, had married around 1429 an obscure Welsh squire called Owen Tudor. According to gossip, he fell drunkenly into her lap at a court function. Owen was beheaded at Hereford after the Battle of Mortimer's Cross in 1461, but he had fathered two sons. The elder, Edmund of Richmond, married Lady Margaret Beaufort, who was descended from John of Gaunt, Duke of Lancaster. This gave Henry Tudor, son of the marriage, his claim to Richard III's crown.

> *'The body of King Richard, naked of all clothing and laid upon a horse's back, was brought to the abbey of the Franciscans at Leicester, a miserable spectacle but not unworthy for the man's life, and there was buried two days after without any pomp or solemn funeral.'*
>
> The Italian chronicler and cleric Polydore Vergil (c. 1470 – c. 1555)

TUDOR ORIGINAL

King Henry VII, by the Italian sculptor Pietro Torrigiano. Henry had useful kingly attributes: he was evasive, cautious, calculating, resolute and ambitious.

ROYAL SURVIVOR

Elizabeth of York was the daughter of Edward IV and Elizabeth Woodville. Her marriage to Henry Tudor united the remnants of the warring parties. Her second son became Henry VIII.

Brought up in Wales, Henry spent 14 years exiled in France before he made his bid for the throne. He had moved too late to take advantage of the Duke of Buckingham's 1483 revolt, for which Buckingham paid with his head. Undiscouraged, in 1485 he landed in Milford Haven with a small army.

Richard led his forces to meet the challenge but apathy and treachery among his supporters decided the result at Bosworth Field on 22 August 1485. Thomas, Lord Stanley (Henry's stepfather), held back from the battle, while his brother Sir William Stanley attacked King Richard at the rear. Richard fought with desperate courage, refusing a horse on which to flee with the grim retort 'that he would that very day make end either of war or life'. He fell, still wearing the crown. Lord Stanley took it from his helmet and placed it on Henry's head.

Henry VII's marriage to Elizabeth of York, daughter of Edward IV, united the warring lines of Lancaster and York. Though discontent and plots rumbled on for some years, the Wars of the Roses were over. The triumphant Tudor dynasty stamped a new emblem, the double rose, on a new age.

MEDIEVAL LIFE

THE LEGACY OF THE MIDDLE AGES includes the ancient castles, cathedrals and parish churches of England. Almost all date from the period after 1066 and the Norman Conquest. The impressive buildings remain, but what of the lives spent in and around them? Place names and family names serve as passwords to a vanished world – of lords and ladies, reeves and squires, clerks, haywards and ploughmen, archers and outlaws. The medieval social structure seems as unyielding as any castle wall. Yet its tiers could be climbed by the clever, the ambitious and the lucky – from even the humblest origins.

For most English men and women, daily life involved grinding, back-breaking work – finding food, making clothes, building and repairing homes. Yet there was fun too: song and poetry, feasting and frolicking, music and merrymaking, hunting and hawking. Medieval families could be large, but many children succumbed to disease. Childhood was often short. Few peasants ever travelled far from the district where they were born; some never left their village.

Their surroundings and way of life changed little over centuries. Yet this apparently humdrum lifestyle was played out against a backdrop of extravagant feasts, tournaments and jousts, regal rituals, fetid towns, moneymaking markets, religious ceremonial and displays of fanatical piety. Medieval England was gaudy, raucous and often glorious. The colours may have faded, but distant echoes linger.

GARDENS FOR PLEASURE AND PLENTY

Gardens gave space within a castle's walls for play and pleasure and for growing the herbs, fruit and vegetables needed for food and medicines.

IGHTHAM MOTE

Ightham Mote in Kent is a moated manor house, little changed externally since it was built in 1340. The name comes from the Old English word 'moot', for meeting place.

HARVEST TIME

Peasants use curve-bladed sickles to harvest wheat. The men are in typical work clothes of short woollen tunic and hose (thigh-length stockings).

ROYAL COURTS AND PARLIAMENTS

ALONE AND ALOOF

Richard II became king at the age of 10. This painting in Westminster Abbey is the earliest-known portrait from life of a medieval king.

NORMAN KINGS OF ENGLAND, and their successors, held on to huge territories in France. They used French as the language of court and government in England, but the 14th-century wars between the two countries eroded the status of 'English French'. After Agincourt (1415), Henry V's campaign reports in English mark a new era for the use of the 'native' language.

Lords and ladies at court, with their fashionable dress, smart talk and elegant entertainments, vied for royal favour. But 'the English', wrote Jean Froissart, the French chronicler, 'will never love and honour a king unless he be victorious and a lover of arms and war.'

Henry II was good at war. He also reorganized the English legal system: government's prime concern under Henry was maintaining good order. Henry III had to live with the legacy of Magna Carta, the set of 'ancient rights' imposed on his father King John by the barons in 1215. In 1258, Henry was forced to pay attention to a barons' council, led by Simon de Montfort. The resulting tensions led to civil war, during which de Montfort summoned a Great Council including not only nobles but also representatives from the shires and towns. This is hailed as the forerunner of England's Parliament, used by later kings to raise money through taxes, with inevitable wranglings significant for the future government of the realm. The assembly summoned by King Edward I in 1295 became known as the Model Parliament, because it foreshadowed later developments.

Democracy had barely been planted. People accepted the inequalities of medieval England in the belief that the hierarchy was ordained by God and needed for peace and prosperity. Supreme on his earthly throne (though not immune from overthrow) sat the king.

The king's immense powers did not always shield him from dangers close to home. In 1173, the three surviving sons of Henry II rebelled against him, aided by their mother. As usual in these cases, the cause was the division of royal lands between the sons. A shrewd king ruled both

his kingdom and his own family with a mixture of fairness and firmness. A king was expected to demonstrate public piety: Henry III gave lavish alms to the poor, feeding 500 hungry paupers every day at his own expense. Above all, a king was expected to win battles, cow foreign enemies and increase the national treasury. If he did this, Parliament was likely to support him and vote the taxation the king might require for the building of palaces and castles, or the arranging of royal weddings.

Royal marriages were the cause of much diplomatic toing and froing. Court officials were sent to look over prospective brides. In 1319, Bishop Stabledon travelled to Flanders to see Philippa of Hainault, future queen of Edward III. He reported that '... in all things she is pleasant enough. And the damsel will be of the age of nine years on St John's day next.'

'Her forehead is high and broad ... her mouth fairly wide, the lower teeth project a little.'

Bishop Stabledon, on Philippa of Hainault, future queen of Edward III

THE KING AND PARLIAMENT

Edward I seated in Parliament. On woolsacks in the middle are the Chancellor (the king's chief minister) and judges. Either side of Edward are the rulers of Scotland and Wales, with the archbishops of Canterbury and York.

CHIVALRY AND TOURNAMENTS

A KNIGHT BELONGED to an elite social group. After rigorous training, he was expected to prove his worth by loyalty, prowess and stamina. No less important was *courtoisie* – a grasp of the manners and refinements of court circles. The 'perfect, gentle knight' had grace, wit, eloquence of speech, skill at games such as chess, and a tuneful voice with which to serenade a fair lady with love songs.

Chivalrous knights were expected to protect women, the poor and the defenceless, to be generous, and to undertake heroic quests – such as going on crusade to the Holy Land. But warfare was the knight's prime business and the tournament was where he tried out his manoeuvres in a stage-managed rehearsal for battlefield mayhem. Shining at a tournament offered a poor, landless knight or younger son the chance to win fame, prizes, royal favour or marriage to a rich heiress.

Tournaments had begun as groups of knights piling into a free-for-all called a mêlée. Defeated (but still breathing) contestants might be ransomed and their horses and armour taken as booty. When mêlées became too violent they were replaced by jousts in which two knights charged at one another with lances, their mounts separated by a wooden barrier. Richard I and Edward I, enthusiastic jousters, laid down tournament rules to prevent outright murder by a knight's followers and brawling with spectators.

21ST-CENTURY KNIGHT

Jousting re-enactments are popular at medieval festivals. Staged combats recreate the drama and muscular skills of medieval knights.

NIGHTS TO REMEMBER

The French chronicler Jean Froissart (c. 1337–1410) had a good time at a Smithfield tournament in 1390. The opening parade featured 60 mounted knights, each led by a lady of rank, herself on horseback. On the next day (Monday) the fun began: '... everyone **exerted himself to the utmost, many were unhorsed,** and many more **lost their helmets.** The jousting continued with great **courage and perseverance** until night put an end to it. The company then retired, and **when supper-time was come, the lords and ladies attended.'**

**AWAITING THE
FIRST BLOW**

*A tournament scene in London.
Ladies pick their favourites as
competing knights parade before
the serious jousting begins.*

Cheating (such as secretly arming a horse with a spiked breastplate to wound an opponent's mount) was condemned as thoroughly unsporting. Plate armour and blunt lances made jousting clashes a little safer, but serious injuries and deaths remained frequent. By 1300 a joust might entail three bouts with lances, three with swords and three with axes – if either man was still on his feet!

A large-scale tournament was much more than a sweaty dust-up between over-muscled heavyweights on horseback. It was a glittering social occasion, attracting overseas competitors and a host of the great and good, all in their best clothes. Lady spectators chose the winners: after the first day of jousting at a Smithfield tournament in 1390, a gold crown was awarded to the best foreign knight, the Count d'Ostrevant, and a consolation prize of a golden clasp went to 'a gallant knight of England, Sir Hugh Spencer'.

Next day at Smithfield there was more jousting by squires (for this less prestigious event, prize-winners were awarded a horse and a falcon). When the day's jousts were ended, the wounded retired to be bathed and bandaged, while everyone else enjoyed supper at the bishop's palace and danced until daybreak. On the third day, the company reassembled to cheer a general set-to 'by all knights and squires indiscriminately'. This grand finale brought the event to a close, but there was still the rest of the week to be spent feasting, praising the victors and commiserating with the equally bruised and battered losers.

HERALDRY

HERALDRY HAD PRACTICAL origins. Knights on the battlefield, encased in armour, needed to know who their friends were. So identifying marks were obviously useful. The simple custom then grew into an elaborate social ritual and art form. In a world where modesty was not much valued, 'coats of arms' made a bold statement: 'This is my family,' 'I hold this office,' even 'I have done these noble deeds.' A knight displayed his merits proudly on his armour, his helmet crest, and on badges worn by his servants. By the 15th century, heraldry had refined rules, and was transformed into a colourful ritual to be enjoyed by all who could afford it.

The shield's broad, flat surface was ideal for displaying a pattern or symbol, called a charge. This could also decorate the garment a knight wore over his armour – the surcoat ('coat of arms') – his horse's caparison (a cloth covering) and his personal banner and flag.

HERALD IN UNIFORM

This illuminated initial from a 1456 grant of arms to the Tallow Chandlers' Company shows a herald, a medieval 'officer of arms'.

ARMS OF WALES'S PRINCE

The arms of Llywelyn, Prince of Wales, who died in 1240, form part of the current arms of HRH The Prince of Wales.

THE ORDER OF THE GARTER

The Order of the Garter, founded according to tradition in 1348, includes the sovereign and 25 men and women, with other members of the royal family. The Garter Knights' banners hang in the choir of St George's Chapel, Windsor.

The Knights Templar   The Knights of St John

CRUSADING ARMS

During the crusades (1071–1291) knights who belonged to a religious order wore crosses on their shields and surcoats.

Coats of arms were devised by officials known as heralds, who kept records to make sure no two families bore the same decoration. Heralds also organized tournaments: the first heralds were probably wandering minstrels, skilled in memorizing heroic tales and identifying knights in combat from their 'strips'.

By the late 14th century, coats of arms were not only used by the wives and daughters of knights, but also by non-military gentry and churchmen as well as towns and corporations, such as the City of London's 'livery companies', or trade guilds.

By the end of the 15th century, developments in arms and armour left less room for personal heraldic display. Soldiers fought beneath a knight's standard or colours. At the Battle of Bosworth (1485), for example, some wore the green and white jackets of the Earl of Richmond's men, others the red jackets of Sir William Stanley's band, and so forth. Heraldry continued to flourish, in the life of town and country rather than on the battlefield, because of its ability to absorb the new, to link with the past and to provide continuity with the present.

Today, heralds are members of the Royal Household and on state occasions they process in short-sleeved coats or 'tabards' bearing the royal arms. The College of Arms was founded by Richard III.

THE LANGUAGE OF HERALDRY

Heraldry has its own language, called blazon. Arising from French and Latin, it describes a coat of arms in a way that leaves no room for confusion. The shield's surface is known as the field. The five colours or tinctures are purpure (purple), sable (black), vert (green), azure (blue) and gules (red). There are two metals: or (gold) and argent (white), and several furs (such as ermine and vair).

The chief

The saltire

The cross

The pale

The chevron

The bend

The bend sinister

ORDINARIES

Simple geometric shapes placed on the shield are known as ordinaries (like those shown here). Shapes and objects, such as animals, are called charges.

Lines of partition, dividing the shield, include checky and quarterly.

The arms of De Warenne (checky)

The arms of De Mandeville (quarterly)

ART AND LETTERS

WRITING AND PAINTING in medieval England were leisurely arts. Alexander Neckham in the 12th century describes the tools of the scribe, usually a monk: 'a knife with which he can shape a quill pen [prepared with the inside fuzzy scale of a feather scraped out] … a boar's or goat's tooth for polishing the parchment, so that the ink of a letter may not run.' Scribes also needed a line marker, a basin of hot coals (to dry the ink) and perhaps a window-screen of linen or parchment, coloured to shade the sunlight – 'green and black offer more comfort to the eyes.'

Book-reading was still for the privileged few, but the eyes of all, great and lowly, could feast on the richness of medieval art and architecture. Early English, Decorated, Perpendicular: these were the three great periods of English medieval architecture that produced towering works to the glory of God. Art was usually religious. It included tomb sculptures and church wall paintings, many of which were destroyed or painted over during the Reformation in the 1500s. But it seems that people also had colourfully painted walls in their homes.

Hours of patient handwork produced objects of staggering beauty: stained glass, silver, gold, jewellery. Goldsmiths ranked above painters in the medieval art world, where craftsmen working in wood, metal and stone also produced work of outstanding quality.

The best-known and most widely read writer of medieval England is Geoffrey Chaucer (*c.* 1340–1400), author of *The Canterbury Tales*, but he was not alone.

THE FATHER OF ENGLISH LITERATURE

Geoffrey Chaucer was a traveller in the royal service in the 1370s, a customs official and, for two years (1389–91), Clerk of the King's Works with a comfortable income. When he gave up this job, after being robbed several times, he concentrated on writing. Chaucer never finished his Canterbury Tales – he planned to bring his pilgrims back to London from Canterbury, adding more tales to the 24 he wrote in the 1390s.

'[Musicians] haunt public drinking and wanton assemblies, where they sing divers songs to move men to wantonness.'

Thomas de Cabham

SINGING MONKS

This 14th-century painted miniature comes from the Litlyngton Missal in Westminster Abbey. The Mass book was the gift of Nicholas Litlyngton, abbot from 1362 to 1386.

His peers included: William Langland (died *c.* 1400), author of the allegory *Piers Plowman*; John Lydgate (died *c.* 1450); and John Gower (died 1408). Although rare, books were evidently not always valued as treasures. Richard de Bury, tutor of Edward III, complained of 'shameless youths who, when they have learned to shape the letters of the alphabet, become incongruous annotators of all the fairest volumes that come their way,' scribbling in the margins 'whatsoever frivolous stuff may happen to run at that moment in their heads.'

There were no theatres, in the modern sense, in medieval England. Troupes of performers went around the streets

68

performing on temporary stages in the open air. Mystery plays, the oldest medieval dramas, were Bible-based stories staged by local traders' guilds. Some survive: the Chester mystery plays are still performed every five years. Morality plays developed from the mysteries, and were more sophisticated, retelling Bible stories with allegorical characters such as Vice, Virtue, Poverty, and the Seven Deadly Sins. Miracle plays depicted the lives of saints.

The Church, which had at first sponsored drama, came to disapprove. Actors, thought the 14th-century churchman Thomas de Cabham, were mostly 'to be damned'. They transfigured their bodies 'by base contortions, or by denuding themselves, or by wearing horrible masks.' Rather than do honest work, they committed criminal deeds or hung around the court. It was permissible to listen to the songs of jongleurs (itinerant minstrels) praising the deeds of princes and the lives of the saints, but as a rule, 'to give to play-actors is no other than to throw our money away.'

IVORY CARVED TO LAST

This ivory carving on a bishop's crozier (1150–70) illustrates the life of St Nicholas. Ivory was an expensive material, imported either from the Baltic (walrus) or the East (elephant). Ideal for delicate carving, ivory was hard and long-lasting.

NORMAN SKILL IN SILVER

The Gloucester candlestick, from Gloucester Cathedral, is a masterpiece of Romanesque art from the early 1100s, during the reign of Henry I.

LOVE AND MARRIAGE

COURTLY LOVE
'Courtly love', inspired by the tales and songs of troubadours, placed women on a pedestal. Here a knight accepts the favours of his lady.

MEDIEVAL MARRIAGE was sometimes for love, but more often (among the landed gentry) for money and estates. Royal marriages were dictated by foreign policy, and it was common for neither party to have seen the other before the ceremony. Ambassadors were sent to do royal wooing, and reported back with approval (or not) of the proposed spouse.

Courtship could be quite formal. In the 15th-century Cely Letters, Richard Cely describes to his family how he went to church to set eyes on the young woman for whom he was intended, both parties being suitably chaperoned. He was invited to dinner (which he declined) but gifts were exchanged – wine from him, a roast heron from the young woman, and after dinner, the pair met and had 'right good communication and the person pleased me well ... she is young, little and very well-favoured and witty and the country speaks much good of her.' There remained the dowry to arrange, and parental consent to the marriage.

Fanciful notions of romance and courtly love might inspire poetry, but Church leaders warned against frivolity. The Bishop of Durham insisted in 1220 that 'marriages be decently celebrated, with reverence, not with laughter and ribaldry, not in taverns or at public drinkings and feastings.' Marriage vows were to be made 'in the presence of a priest and of three or four respectable persons summoned for the purpose.'

Chaucer's Wife of Bath had had five husbands 'all at the church door, apart from other company in youth', and

ON THE MOVE

Royal ladies take to the road. Wagons carried household goods and furnishings from castle to manor house during the regular 'progresses' that medieval rulers made around their domains.

marriage guidance was as frequent and varied as it is today. Men were warned that rich wives did not necessarily bring happiness. Mothers were advised to discipline their children, especially boys who 'make a ceaseless noise and endless chatter ... As soon as they have been washed, they make themselves filthily dirty' (from the encyclopedic writings of Bartholomaeus Anglicus, *c.* 1240, translated from Latin to English by John Trevisa in 1398).

A happy marriage could survive the turbulence of civil war, separation and family misfortunes. The Paston Letters, written by members of a Norfolk family, cover the years 1422 to 1509, during the Wars of the Roses. In 1465, Margaret Paston wrote from Norwich to her husband John, who was in London, enmeshed in lawsuits. She asked him to buy three yards of dress material of 'what colour pleaseth you, for in good faith I have done all the drapers' shops in this town and here is right feeble choice.' She also requested he buy 'a loaf of good sugar and half a pound of whole cinnamon, for there is none good in this town.'

WEDDING CHESTS

Medieval homes were sparsely furnished by modern standards. Family valuables were locked in stout wooden chests, like this rather splendid one.

FURNISHING THE BEDROOM

'In the bedchamber, let a curtain go around the walls decently, or a scenic canopy, for the avoiding of flies and spiders.' For added comfort, Alexander Neckham suggests a feather mattress, with a quilted pad for the head, sheets of muslin or linen, and for winter warmth coverlets of woollen cloth or blankets lined with the fur of badger, cat, beaver or sable. For bedroom furniture: a chair, stool and bench, together with a pole for hanging clothing and another pole **'on which can rest a hawk'.**

71

FEASTS AND FESTIVALS

ROYAL FEAST

This painting of the 1400s shows a king dining in state. The meat, served by a ladle-wielding servant from a side-table (left), is carried to the table while a musician plays (right).

WHEN A GREAT HOUSEHOLD partied, an army of servants bustled into action. No expense was spared, nor edible bird or beast – from lark to swan. In 1251, when Henry III's daughter Margaret married Alexander, king of Scots, the bread bill alone came to £7,000.

⤴

Meals were served in the great hall. The king, or lord, sat raised on a dais at the high table, with his family and close companions. The company sat in the body of the hall at trestle-tables. Contrary to popular belief, medieval feasts were seldom rowdy or brutish. Diners washed before and after each

meal, and there was no hurling of half-gnawed bones to hunting dogs – at least, not in polite society. Manners were rather refined, white linen cloths covered the tables and though people ate mainly with their fingers (forks came later), there were strict rules for table etiquette. Dipping dirty fingernails into a communal dish was frowned upon, as were talking with the mouth full and putting unwiped, greasy lips to a shared cup. Commonly, people ate off trenchers – slices of poor quality bread. Only a glutton or 'trencher-man' would eat his trencher; the bread-plates were usually collected and passed on to the poor.

Breakfast does not seem to have been a common meal. People had dinner around 10 a.m. (having been up since 5), and sat down to supper at 5 or 6 p.m. when the day's work ended. Clock-time, of course, was still to come.

The main festivals of the medieval year were seasonal and religious. Sunday was a day of rest, and meat was not eaten on Fridays. There were numerous saints' days throughout the year, but Easter was the most important holiday in the Church calendar. People also enjoyed Christmas, with its mid-winter celebrations of pagan origins, and its banquet, at which the Yule boar (or pig-shaped pie for the less well-off) was the central dish. Margaret Paston in 1459 describes quiet Christmas games of backgammon, chess and cards in the house of a friend in mourning. There were no 'disguisings [play-acting or mumming], harping, luting or singing, nor any lewd sports' – all part of the festive fun in happier homes!

KITCHEN EQUIPMENT

Family letters list the kitchen goods of the Paston family's neighbour, the soldier Sir John Fastolf (whose property the Pastons inherited after his death in 1459). These included **'1 great brass pot,** 1 frying pan, sundry smaller pots, 3 pike pans, 1 cauldron, 1 gridiron, 2 spits of varying sizes, 1 mortar and pestle, **1 wooden sieve** or colander, 1 pair of tongs, **1 strainer and a vinegar bottle'.**

MEDIEVAL DINING HALL

The Great Hall of Winchester Castle. The hall of a great house made a splendid backdrop for feasts. Every important house and castle had such a hall, the focal point of life and entertaining guests.

A HUNTING PICNIC

Huntsmen enjoy a rather elaborate forest picnic, in this mid-14th-century painting.

MUSIC AND MERRYMAKING

MUSIC, ENJOYED BOTH at court and the ale-house, was also part of church worship. Most songs or 'carols' were never written down – although the best-known medieval song in English, *Sumer is icumen in,* was probably written in the early 1200s, as a round for four voices.

Most music in medieval times was 'monophonic', with a single melody line, but 'polyphony' (in motets, for example) became popular. Stringed instruments included the harp, the psaltery (which developed into the dulcimer), the lute, the gittern (a small lute) and the fiddle. There were numerous wind instruments: the trumpet, shawm, bombard, bagpipe and organ, while rhythm sections included small drums, tabor, timbre (tambourine), cymbals, bells, clappers and rattles.

Everyone danced, from peasant to king, in a stately court measure or exuberant country jig. Minstrels had jobs in great houses, paid to play background music at dinner or at bath-time, or to while away the night hours for insomniacs. They also performed at functions ranging from family weddings to celebrations as lavish as Edward I's Feast of the Swans in 1306. On that occasion, among an army of minstrels and entertainers was the king's favourite dancer, Matilda Makejoy. Although listed as a paid minstrel in Royal Household records for 1306, she was in reality an acrobatic dancer who probably cavorted nude.

PUTTING ON THE GREEN
People liked dressing up. Knights clanked about pretending to be characters from Arthurian legend, and this picture of about 1390 shows the dance of the wodehouses, mythical creatures of the woods.

An acrobatic dancer (right) could never have performed in such heavy clothing. The artist-monk who illustrated this Bible scene may have given the dancer a long dress for modesty.

Jesters told stories and jokes, often rude and satirical. A rather surprising royal performer was Roland Le Fartere, whose act lived up to his name and so delighted

Henry I that he gave him a house and grounds in Suffolk.

Jesters took liberties, but could get themselves into trouble. It is said that the pious Henry III was delighted to hear his jester compare him to Christ. When pressed to explain, the jester told him that according to the teachings of the Church, Christ was as wise at birth as he was at the age of 30. The same was true of Henry, who knew as much at the age of 30 as he had when a newborn infant – not perhaps what the king expected to be told! Rash jesters usually managed to talk themselves out of tight spots and get away with their heads, if not a generous tip from a less-than-amused master.

Minstrels were all-round entertainers, with a repertoire of songs, instrumental playing, tumbling, juggling, stilt-dancing, or performing with animals. Towns employed town bands, known as waits, who also acted as watchmen and blew loud blasts on their trumpets to raise the alarm as required.

PERFORMING MINSTRELS

This decorated letter shows minstrels performing. Henry V took musicians with him to his French wars. He paid them 12 pennies a day, twice as much as an archer.

'[The Welsh] do not sing in unison … but in many different parts … you will hear as many different parts and voices as there are performers, who all at length unite.'

Gerald the Welshman,
c. 1146–c. 1220

75

HUNTING, HAWKING AND BOISTEROUS SPORTS

STAGS AT BAY

Stags were stalked by stealth and pursued with hounds. Here two huntsmen close in on their quarry with bows.

HUNTING WAS THE MOST absorbing pastime for all great men, and for many lesser men, and women, too. Still largely covered by dense forest and wilderness, England was the haunt of deer, wild boar and wolves. Norman kings reserved about a third of the country as their hunting ground, protected by draconian laws, as a means of protecting the game and reserving the best sport for themselves. The forest law made life difficult for people living there, since even cutting wood might be 'interfering' with the animals. Forest wardens or verderers had grim penalties at their disposal, and the tales of Robin Hood remind us of what could happen to a poor man hunting the king's deer.

HUNTING TOGETHER

A lord and lady ride out to enjoy the pleasures of falconry.

76

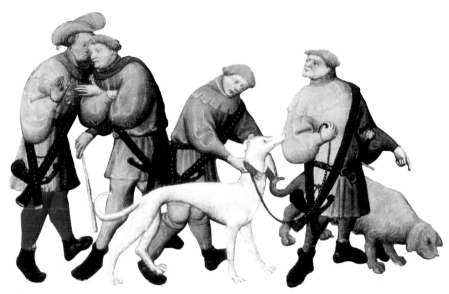

HUNTING DOGS

England had been renowned for its hunting dogs since pre-Roman times. In the Middle Ages, huntsmen used a variety of breeds including greyhounds, deerhounds, wolfhounds, mastiffs and terriers.

'Many of the citizens [of London] delight in taking their sport with birds of the air, merlins and falcons and the like, and with dogs that wage warfare in the woods.' William Fitzstephen, c. 1180

Hunters generally rode on horseback, armed with bow or spear. Hawks and falcons were used to hunt all sorts of birds including pigeon, duck and heron. Falconry was regarded as a noble art. It was a sign of high rank to carry a hawk on the wrist, even when attending church. Favourite birds had pride of place on perches around the hall and even in the bedchamber. Hunting dogs and trophies were much in evidence: a lord's hall was likely to be 'strewed with marrow bones, full of hawks' perches, hounds, spaniels and terriers ... hung with the fox skins of this and last year's hunting.'

Sports were muscular, rowdy and rough: stone-throwing, quarter-staff, quoits, horseshoe-tossing, bowls, wrestling, and sword and buckler fights (using wooden swords and shields). For stoolball, women sat on milking stools and tried to dodge balls that were thrown by men. Football, or campball, sometimes brought together rival villages, with goals set a mile apart, scores of players, and much off-the-ball confrontation.

MEAT FOR THE POT

Rabbits were reared in warrens, protected from predators, to provide fresh meat. Flushed out with small dogs and ferrets, they were captured in nets.

77

COSTUME

DRESSED FOR ETERNITY

A memorial brass of 1487 in Heyford, Northamptonshire, shows an armoured knight and his lady, looking their best for posterity.

ELEGANT LADY

A lady in her garden. As in every age, the rich celebrated their status by leading fashion; the dress of the poor hardly changed from one century to the next.

IN MEDIEVAL ENGLAND it was clothes (rather than manners) that made the man – or woman. Peasants wore more or less the same, year in, year out – a loose tunic of coarse wool with thigh-length stockings (hose) tied to the underwear (braies, a kind of loincloth). Women wore loose dresses with aprons. A hood and cloak or mantle, or an old sack for the beggar, kept off the rain and wind.

Most people wore a linen chemise or undershirt, although ascetic monks put on hairshirts to chasten the flesh. On top of undershirts went tunics and gowns. Most dress was utilitarian, although late 14th-century male fashions were more extravagant, with multi-coloured outfits and absurdly pointed shoes. In extreme cases, the wearer had to fix chains from his knees to the toes of his shoes to avoid tripping over his feet.

Bright colours, silks and satins were worn only by the rich, and among those the men dressed more gaudily than the women. Women wore their hair long, but covered with a veil or headdress, such as the steepling wimple. Another remarkable piece of headgear was the liripipe, a long hood with a point that wound around the neck and hung down to the knees. The academic dress hood worn by university graduates is said to derive from this.

Furs were worn for winter warmth, and for showy competition by the lordly, who sported robes of vair (the grey-blue and white pelts of the Baltic squirrel), sable, fox and even wolf. A ruling of 1281 forbade common women in London to wear fur other than lamb or rabbit, since 'nurses, servants and women of loose life bedizen themselves and wear hoods furred with great vair and miniver squirrel in guise of good ladies.'

Servants were told to 'see that your lord has a clean shirt and hose, a short coat, a doublet, and a long coat, if he wears such, his hose well brushed, his socks at hand.' A servant helped his master dress, warming linen by the fire on chilly mornings, combing the noble hair and providing water for washing the face and hands. He brought gown, cap and cloak 'all clean and nice' before the master left home.

FASHION ICON

Elizabeth Woodville, queen of Edward IV, was a fashion icon of the mid-1400s. This portrait conveys her cool, rather calculating elegance.

RELAXING IN SUMMER

People kept themselves well covered even on a summer's day, though nudity (when swimming, for example) raised few eyebrows.

TOWN AND COUNTRY

ALFRISTON CLERGY HOUSE

Built for a parish priest about 1350, Alfriston Clergy House in East Sussex was the first property acquired by The National Trust, in 1896.

WE PLOUGH THE FIELDS AND SCATTER

Ploughing, sowing and harvesting: the country year's seasonal tasks, for men and women.

ENGLAND'S LAND WAS GREEN and pleasant, with little sign of invasive humans apart from a few twists of woodsmoke, strips of ploughed land in fields, a distant spire or the looming grey outline of a castle.

Society in medieval England was almost wholly rural. In 1066, the population of England was probably about two million – smaller than that of Roman Britain. By the 1300s, the population had more than doubled. Towns flourished, some old Roman towns, others new (Leeds, Liverpool, Chelmsford). Even so, only 1 in 20 persons lived in a town, which would be, by modern standards, tiny. London was easily the biggest city, with around 50,000 inhabitants. Its northern rival, York, had fewer than 8,000.

Most people stayed for life in the town, village or tiny hamlet where they had been born, or where work or marriage had taken them. Few English people saw much of their own country, except the king (who travelled most of the time), merchants, travelling entertainers, judges and tax collectors. Travel was often dangerous. Roads were impassable in rain and snow, and while danger haunted town alleys, the unknown lay hidden along greenwood pathways: 'For therein wild beasts are hunted. There is the place of hiding and of lurking, for often in woods thieves be hid.' John Trevisa's 13th-century advice to travellers is to follow 'road-signs', such as knotted rags on trees and bushes marking the highway, but to beware, since thieves 'change such knots and signs and beguile many men and bring them out of the right way.'

ENGLAND'S VINTAGE

This scene of hoeing and pruning in a vineyard confirms that winemaking was a flourishing activity in England. Evidence suggests that the country enjoyed a mild climate for much of the Middle Ages.

MEDIEVAL HUMOUR

Townspeople were already starting to make fun of slow-witted country bumpkins. Around the fire, they enjoyed cracking jokes – many, no doubt, already old. Among the first jokes printed – by Wynken de Worde, assistant to William Caxton – were these dating from the late 1400s:

'What thing is it that hath no end?... A bowl.'

'What is it that never freezeth?... Hot water.'

'What thing is it, the less it is the more it is dreaded?... A bridge.'

WORKING THE LAND

HAYMAKING TIME

Cutting hay with scythes. The man on the far left uses a stone to sharpen the blade; the man next to him wields a pitchfork.

GREAT COXWELL BARN

The tithe barn at Great Coxwell in Berkshire was built in the 13th century by the monks of Beaulieu. Such barns were used to store the tithe, the annual levy on farmers' crops.

THE ENGLISH were a mixture of farmers, shepherds, smiths, wheelwrights, wagonwrights and ditch-diggers. Most could be described as peasants (country people). Some were quite prosperous freemen, forerunners of the Tudor yeoman farmer; others were humble serfs or cottars (cottagers).

Serfs, or villeins, could not in theory own property, since they themselves were chattels of their lords. A grasping lord could take whatever he liked from them, arguing that villeins were not entitled to own anything 'except their bellies'. Fortunately for serfs, the 'custom of the manor' dictated that the son of a deceased tenant

FARM FARE

In William Langland's poem *Piers Plowman* (c. 1370), country foods mentioned include geese, piglets, green (new) cheese, curds, cream, oaten cake, loaves of beans and bran, salt bacon, parsley, leeks, peas, cabbages, cherries, pears and baked apples, as well as harvest treats of fresh brown ale and bread made with new, white flour. Farmers grew wheat, rye, barley and oats.

FEEDING THE SWINE
A swineherd shakes down acorns from a coppiced oak to feed his pigs; from a manuscript of the 12th century.

could 'inherit' his father's land on payment of a fine and the handing over of a heriot (death duty) – usually his best cow or something of similar value. With dues paid and obligations met, few villeins were likely to be obstructed by a master whose main interest was the continued prosperity of his estate.

Village life was communal, and peasant families ran their smallholdings as cooperatives. They grew vegetables on their own plots, grazing pigs and cattle on the common land. They could also find work on local estates, as bailiffs' records reveal. Dereham Abbey's accounts for 1366 show 'for wage of one man mending collars and gear of a cart for 2 days 10d. [10 pennies] ... for 1 man hired at 3d. a day for 4 days to wash and hang herrings 13d. ... for mowing and binding half an acre of wheat 7d.' The same record tells us that the farm sold two cows for 30 shillings, 2 pigs for 16 shillings and bought a plough for just 13 pennies (though various parts were extra).

A tract written about 1289 tells ploughmen to be 'full of song' to encourage their oxen and to treat the beasts well, grooming, feeding and even sleeping with them when the day's work was done. Shepherds should be 'intelligent and watchful', with 'a good barking dog' – and while farming has changed much since the Middle Ages, the shepherd has worked through the centuries with his dog, crook and lambing hurdles right up to modern times.

LIFE AND DEATH IN THE TOWNS

DEATH OF A QUEEN

Queen Anne, wife of Richard II, died of the plague in 1394. The disease spread easily in towns, where people lived close together in unsanitary conditions.

CRAFTSMAN AT WORK

Craftsmen clustered in back-street workshops, producing assorted sounds and smells as they made pottery, leatherwork, metal goods, cloth and (shown in this reconstruction) wooden cups, turned on a lathe.

MEDIEVAL TOWNS GREW when well sited to act as markets for local trade or centres of local government. The weekly market was the highpoint of local life, a chance to buy and sell anything from a basket of eggs to a horse. Tradesmen worked in streets or districts assigned to them – hence the Shambles ('slaughterhouses') for butchers in York and the streets with 'trade names' – Baker, Fish, Poultry, Cornhill, Smith, Haymarket, Tanner – in many old towns.

Even so, towns were small. In 1400, perhaps only five (London, York, Bristol, Coventry and Norwich) had more than 1,000 houses. Most were like large villages, in which farm animals and vermin roamed freely. Many were walled; some had harbours or bridges or a castle. They had law courts, mints, churches and schools, developing for the most part higgledy-piggledy. Streets were narrow and dirty, with open drains. Houses were usually wood-and-plaster structures, with thatched roofs. More substantial stone houses (some of which survive) testified to their owner's prosperity.

❧

Larger towns took pride and profit from a royal charter that granted both the title of 'borough' and trading privileges. Prosperous groups of traders and craft-workers set up trade guilds to protect the rights of their members. Guilds were supposed to uphold standards, but customer complaints of dishonest trading – especially by bakers, butchers, cooks and brewers – were many. Writing in the 1380s, the poet John Gower warned readers against smooth-talking, slippery salesmen 'full of artifice, of joking and nonsense, to make fools of silly people so as to get their money – chalk for cheese he can sell you.'

❧

To medieval moralists, the town was a place of entertainment and temptation – where innocent and goodly country folk

were liable to be bemused and dazzled, and sent home penniless. Its streets were full of pickpockets, thieves, con men and women of easy virtue, all waiting to prey on the unwary. Taverns offered the traditional temptations to those unable to curb their appetites – or their thirst. In William Langland's *Piers Plowman*, Glutton visits a London tavern, staying 'till evensong' by which time he had gulped down 'a gallon and a gill' of ale, with predictable results.

'*[Glutton] could neither step nor stand till he had his staff ... his eyes grew dim, he stumbled on the threshold and fell flat on the floor.*'

William Langland, Piers Plowman

ANCIENT TOWN HOUSE

The so-called Jew's House (left) in Lincoln dates from the late 12th century. It was built for a local businessman and is claimed to be the oldest domestic dwelling in England.

LONDON LIFE

LONDON'S ARMS

The City of London's arms date from the mid-14th century. The sword is St Paul's, though popularly supposed to be the dagger used by Lord Mayor Sir William Walworth (a Fishmonger) to stab Wat Tyler, leader of the 1381 Peasants' Revolt.

LONDON'S RIVER

This 15th-century illustration shows the Thames, London's thriving waterway. Barges and small craft pass by the huge keep of the Tower, then painted white (hence 'White Tower').

THE SCOTTISH POET William Dunbar (*c.* 1460–*c.* 1520) called London 'the flower of cities all'. Half the size of Paris – and no match in scale or splendour for Rome or Milan – London was yet the jewel in England's crown. Royal charters recognized its special status, for England's rulers knew that rowdy, rich, threateningly rebellious Londoners were essential allies in any power struggle.

London still had much of its ancient Roman wall, and gates through which daily business ebbed and flowed. Shipping crowded the River Thames. The city's great buildings were its churches, notably St Paul's Cathedral and Westminster Abbey, its several castles, now gone, and the Tower. Despite rubbish-strewn streets, stinking drains and myriad smells, the city entranced most visitors, especially when in pomp and pageantry – such as the mayor's visit to Westminster or the maypole dancing on May Day. City guilds (Goldsmiths, Skinners, Weavers, Saddlers, Fishmongers, etc), presented mystery and miracle plays, the actors appearing on street-corner stages or on carts trundled around the streets. For a coronation, the city celebrated with costumed tableaux, parades of knights and dignitaries, music, food, and conduits flowing with free wine.

↩

Nobles and merchants vied to build and extend town houses, with secluded gardens. They installed modern refinements – stone fireplaces and windows with glass – and imported rugs for floors and tapestries for walls. Prudent householders sited kitchen, brewhouse and dairy in outbuildings, to reduce fire-risk. Fire was a common hazard. After two serious outbreaks, London's sheriff in 1189 ordered stone walls to be built between adjoining wooden houses, and stone or tiled roofs to replace thatch. This reduced, but did not end, the risk of the city going up in flames.

WHITTINGTON'S SHIELD

The City of London's most famous Lord Mayor was Dick Whittington. A cloth merchant first elected in 1398, he acted as banker and moneylender to both Henry IV and Henry V.

OFF TO THE TOWER

King Richard II is led into the Tower of London. While captive, Richard was persuaded to resign the Crown, leaving the throne vacant for Henry Bolingbroke (later Henry IV).

UNPAID BILLS

In London in 1380, Robert Passeleive, a knight, was summoned for unpaid grocer's bills. Sir Robert owed £6 for **'pepper, saffron, ginger, cloves, dates, almonds, rice, cinnamon, figs, raisins, myrrh and other spices'**, for which he had not paid 'though often required'.

GETTING AN EDUCATION

LITERACY MAY NOT have been widespread, but it is wrong to suppose that the only people in medieval England who could read and write were a few monks. There were schools in parish churches, schools in cathedrals and monasteries, guild schools and grammar schools (for teaching Latin grammar, Latin being the Europe-wide language of scholarship).

Schooling in medieval England was sometimes accompanied by harsh beatings. Guibert de Nogent, a monastic writer, must have been relieved when his mother paid his teacher extra money not to beat him. The boy was beaten nevertheless and, when questioned, showed his mother the bruises. Weeping, she vowed he would go to school no more if learning letters required such punishment. He insisted he wanted to go on with his lessons; she reluctantly agreed, on condition that he could give up school and become a knight, when of age, if he so chose.

Some pupils never got farther than the alphabet and Ten Commandments, but others learned Latin composition and translation. Most teachers were clergymen, and their pupils almost all boys, though a few girls went to local schools and others were taught at home. Even poor children could reach the top by study. William of Wykeham (1324–1404, from Wickham in Hampshire) was a clever boy from a very poor family whose

HENRY VI'S SCHOOL
Henry VI was inspired by William of Wykeham's example to found a school. The king's vision was on a grand scale and, though unfinished in his lifetime, Eton College became one of England's most famous educational institutions.

88

education at Winchester's old grammar school was paid for by wealthy patrons. Later a bishop and Edward III's most trusted counsellor, he founded both New College, Oxford, and Winchester School.

England's most famous public school, Eton College, was founded in 1440 by the scholar-king Henry VI but its oldest universities predate that by many years. Oxford University began in the 1100s as a gathering of students around popular teachers: the buildings came later. Modelled on the university at Paris, students hired their teachers, chose their courses and lodged together. The lodgings evolved into colleges, the first being University College (1249). Frequent fights broke out between 'town and gown' (townspeople and students), and it is said that students fleeing violence in Oxford founded England's second-oldest university, Cambridge. Its oldest college is Peterhouse (1284).

King's College, Cambridge, was founded by Henry VI in 1441. Its students were expected to walk 'modestly and without confusion'. Their dress code forbade red or green stockings, pointed shoes or striped hoods, long hair or beards. Nor were they to keep 'dogs, hunting or fishing nets, ferrets, falcons or hawks ... nor any ape, bear, fox, stag, hind, fawn or badger, or any other such ravening or unaccustomed strange beast.'

COLLEGE CALM

The Old Court of Corpus Christi College, Cambridge, dates from 1352. The college is unique among those of Oxford and Cambridge in being founded by townspeople.

DIVINE CALLING

Oxford's Divinity School, paid for by public subscription, was built between 1420–80. Its astonishing fan-vaulted ceiling is studded with 455 carved bosses featuring subscribers' coats of arms and monograms, as well as beasts and biblical images.

CITIES OF ENGLAND

No city in England could rival London in size or importance, but each was proud of its distinctive character. Cathedral cities such as Durham, Lincoln, Exeter, Gloucester, Salisbury, Winchester, York and Norwich were centres of commerce as well as religious worship. Churches dominated the skyline: Norwich had 56 churches within its walls, many built to reflect the wealth of local landowners. Towns flourished near river-crossings, or where two roads met, or where a rich abbey prospered.

ANCIENT GATEWAY IN YORK'S WALLS

Monk Bar is one of four main gateways in York's medieval walls. Figures carved on the towers are poised to drop stones on the enemy below.

DIZZY HEIGHTS OF DURHAM'S TOWER
A head for heights is needed to climb the 325 steps of Durham Cathedral's massive tower, completed around 1490.

Town life was rarely without incident. Civil war called citizens to arms; border towns in the north braced themselves for raids by the Scots. Disputes between traders, arguments over taxes and regulations – rage could quickly lead to riot. In 1355, a brawl erupted in Oxford after a student threw a wine jug at an innkeeper. In the ensuing three-day battle, 63 students were killed and many injured.

Towns developed robust identities, through trade guilds, and through developing local government, presided over by the mayor. But jealously guarded privileges and fierce local pride were not always enough to impress urbane visitors. Richard of Devizes commented acidly in 1204: 'Rochester and Chichester are mere villages ... York abounds in rascals ... Ely is putrefied by the surrounding marshes ... in Durham, Norwich and Lincoln you will never hear anyone speak French ... at Bristol there is nobody who is not, or has not been, a soap-maker [an odiously smelly trade].' Only Winchester was praised: for its gentle monks, its learned clergy, its 'citizens of civility and good faith, its ladies of such beauty and modesty'.

The York roundly abused by Richard of Devizes regarded itself as England's second city. Its Minster, the largest medieval Gothic church in northern Europe, has stood largely unchanged since 1472 (though damaged by fires, the last in 1984).

AN INN NO MORE
The New Inn in Oxford's Cornmarket Street was built in 1389, but it is now occupied by shops.

TRADE AND INDUSTRY

COUNTING THE MONEY

The Exchequer at work: the king watches as coins are weighed. The Exchequer began around 1110, in the reign of Henry I, as a twice-yearly treasury audit of sheriffs' accounts. The calculations were made on a chequered cloth – hence the name.

ENGLAND GREW WEALTHY on sheep. Wool was its chief export, and the wool trade together with cloth-weaving enriched provincial cities such as Norwich. Norwich had a church for every week in the year and – it was said – the city had a pub for every day! Of the 130 or so trades followed there in the 14th century, weaving was the most important.

Because roads were so poor, goods were carried by boat wherever possible. Medieval York was an international port, with ships sailing along the River Ouse and out into the North Sea. Towns came to noisy life on market day, when traders arrived to sell their wares, villagers tramped in to gawp at street entertainers, and swindlers tried to fleece them.

ONE OUT, ALL OUT

In 1484 the bakers of Coventry went on strike. The *Coventry Leet Book* records that in December that year, the bakers **'in great number riotously disposed,** assembled them and unlawfully conferred ... [then] **suddenly departed out of the said city** unto Bakynton [Baginton], **leaving the city destitute of bread.'** The disgruntled bread-makers seem quickly to have changed their minds, as talks with the city's mayor were followed by fines for their misdemeanours.

Animals driven into town for sale added to the dust and cacophony. Chester, like other towns, had more than one livestock market: one near the Northgate and another in the square outside what is now the Town Hall. Many town houses were also business premises. The cellar, or undercroft, served as shop or warehouse, while the hall above provided the main living quarters, with private rooms on the top floor.

Every craft had its own guild, whose members in effect ran the town and, in bouts of enthusiastic altruism, used their money to build guildhalls, almshouses, churches, towers and schools. Merchants who grew wealthy on trade profits could aspire to social equality with a knight. Some merchants (Dick Whittington, for instance) came from noble families; others moved into the aristocracy through marriage. Geoffrey Boleyn, Lord Mayor of London in 1457–58, married a baron's daughter. His great-granddaughter, Anne Boleyn, was to marry a king (Henry VIII).

GUARDING THE CITY

Trading cities were defended by stout walls, gates and castles. Clifford's Tower in York, built by Henry III between 1244 and 1270, is the only remaining part of York Castle.

ADVENTURERS' HALL

The Merchant Adventurers of York built this fine building between 1357 and 1361. One of the best-preserved medieval guildhalls in Europe, it had a hospital and chapel in the undercroft.

LEGACY OF THE MIDDLE AGES

ARUNDEL CASTLE

Arundel's castle rises magnificently on a hill overlooking the river and town. The present building stands on the site of a Norman motte-and-bailey castle erected about 1068.

THE MIDDLE AGES LEFT a rich legacy in art, architecture, literature, landscape and legend. During this time, the English language evolved from various regional dialects into a more-or-less common tongue, the language of Shakespeare. Unified by language, the land was also welded together by laws and customs, many of which survive as the basis for the society we live in today.

Though few houses of ordinary people have survived the centuries, castles can still be seen in many regions of England and Wales. Some remain homes, others are empty and ruinous, but all are worth a visit for each has its own story to tell. The great cathedrals are famous, but many smaller, lesser-known churches also contain gems of medieval art and architecture that are often more accessible and visible. Even more surprisingly, in the age of the car, a few towns and cities still preserve patches of their ancient medieval street patterns, as well as street names which tell of long-vanished trades.

AN ENGLISHMAN'S HOME

Stokesay Castle in Shropshire was originally a manor house, but in 1290 the owner was granted a 'licence to crenellate' (fortify) it. The result was a 'halfway house' between a family home and a castle.

INDEX